Speyers
p.147.

Cambon's post-Diaghilev
party 215-6.

Beecham p.191.
Serbs & Irish p.196.
Nijinsky on Beecham, p.205-6.

MUSIC AT MIDNIGHT

The Angel Between the Piano and the Music Shelves Is *Not* the Russian-Irish Mystic. The Three Lonely Objects on Top of the Music Shelves Are All that Remained of the Canton Enamel

MUSIC AT MIDNIGHT

>>>>>>>>>>>>>>>>>>>>>><<<<<<<<<<<<<<<<<<<<

By

MURIEL DRAPER

ILLUSTRATED

Harper & Brothers Publishers

NEW YORK AND LONDON

1929

MUSIC AT MIDNIGHT

~~~~~~~

TO

MY SONS

PAUL

AND

SANDERS

DRAPER

Contents

Illustrations

Foreword

THE people and events I write of in this book are part of my life. In giving them shape I have depended on the order of their emergence from my memory. I have had no source save the persistence of life, images and sounds in the ever-changing chemistry of time. Whatever inaccuracy of detail or chronological confusion this process may have engendered, will not, I trust, deprive them of an essential truthfulness.

MURIEL DRAPER

MUSIC AT MIDNIGHT

Florence
1909-1911

WHEN I CAME TO LONDON
in the summer of 1911, I left behind me two enchanted
Italian years. The living event of them was the birth of
my son. The geographical centre of them was Florence.
As I reach to capture them, they fade into a background
across which a few vivid figures parade.

I see " Carlo " Loeser pacing haſtily down the narrow
ſtreets that cut into the ſteep Arcetri hillsides on his way
to do battle with Bernard Berenson, freshly descended
from Settignano into the Piazza — any Piazza where
Loeser might find him. Guelph and Ghibelline fought
each other no less valiantly, though with more bloodshed,
than these fervently disagreeing art-taſters. The *casus belli*
varied. It would be the roseate curves of an apple painted
by Cézanne and owned by Loeser, or butchered buttocks
painted by Matisse and bought by " B. B." Or it might
be the feather tip of a wing wafted on to canvas by
the magic of a Malsona di Pietro that aroused Berenson's perverse admiration, or a few precious flakes of
paint let fall to the floor from the archaic folds of a Cimabue saint that inflamed Loeser's enthusiasm. In any case,
Cimabue or Cézanne, Matisse or even a Pietro, they dis-
agreed. Brilliantly. Loeser, somewhat subdued by marriage, paternity, and music, sallies forth less belliger-

3

ently of late years. An occasional reluctant trip to New York, an hour's conversation there with Elizabeth Marbury, his eyes averted from the danger of catching sight from her drawing-room windows of the emporium founded by his forefathers across the East River, a painfully just appraisal of our museums, a polished malediction upon our civilization, and then the eager return to the delights offered of a life amid Arcetri hills, welcomed by music from one of the most perfect string quartets in Europe, whose members live in permanent bliss under his friendly roof.*

A Lorenzo de' Medici from Brooklyn!

Berenson, less dedicated than of yore to the seductive antagonisms aroused by writing astutely of art-tasting, sits talking at Settignano. With a Caligula gesture, he scatters conversational gold pieces into the market-place and watches the few privileged listeners scramble for them. These fortunate few usually make a book apiece out of the nuggets thus acquired and it would be interesting to discover how many of the books written in England during one year could be traced to his intellectual largesse.

I can see timid Americans and tired Florentines sitting about in a magnificent white, gold, and yellow brocade music-room of Mrs. Spaulding's sombre palace on the Lung' Arno, listening to the fine musical performances of her son Albert on the violin. Nothing timid about Mrs. Spaulding's mother, Mrs. Boardman, who suffered the

* Carlo Loeser did not return to the beloved hills from his last visit to New York. He died here in the spring of this year, 1928.

music nobly until such time as she could take her place at the head of the supper table and command the butlers in execrable Italian but with magisterial firmness. I have heard one of the timid American ladies question her about one of the tired Florentines, a princess of sorts. To the American a princess was a legendary and romantic figure, incredibly remote (this was 1910), and she wanted to make her " come true." She asked many awestruck questions which Mrs. Boardman answered with increasing cynicism. And then, after a pause, a wistful, hopeful, " Does she live with her husband, the Prince? " came faltering from the American lady's lips.

" When she gets a chance! " snapped Mrs. Boardman, turning furiously to the butler with a vehement " Giuseppe — *una tasse* — champagne. *Subito!"* and to her grandson, " Albert, some Bach, *quick!* "

Mr. Spaulding made occasional bewildered visits to his family, contributing to the robust and generous atmosphere which made their house an oasis of kind stability in the shifting sophisticated morass of Florentine-American society. Bless them. And one thing more about that house. Tucked away in a far corner of one of the rarely used state drawing-rooms was a small painting of a white, very American-looking spaniel, every hair accurately represented and a blue satin ribbon tied in a bow under its chin. There were moments when I would have taken that painting in preference to the Matisse buttocks or a Cimabue saint.

The Braggiottis! They halt the parade for a moment. Imagine a man who carried in his veins, through some vagary of fate, a stream of pure New England blood mixed with a murky Turkish strain. Then imagine a woman who was born from the union of a bourgeois German Jew to a highly civilized great lady of France. Having accomplished this difficult feat, contemplate for a moment the progeny this combination might produce, and you will begin to approach the Braggiotti phenomena.

Lily Braggiotti divorced one husband to become the wife of Isadore, after which they settled in Florence, Isadore to teach singing and Lily to teach life. These details are presented to suggest a background for the variety of race and upbringing combined in these two people, a combination which imbued the many children subsequently born to them with devastating strains of conflicting talents.

Lily Braggiotti herself was a beautiful, serene figure standing on the shore of life, holding herself as a clear vessel through which life itself could pass into living, finally submerged at high tides by its prolific waters. She now lies beautiful, calm, and dead, having allowed life to be born from her body nine times and at the ninth time bravely carrying herself to other shores. Her zeal for life and birth was the predominating interest of her existence. All young people should marry and have children — in any case have children. An Italian chambermaid could arrive with a sobbing narrative of exaggerated fidelity to her *bello* and be sure of a delighted welcome in the Braggiotti *ménage*. The drivers of the little Florentine fiacres could grossly overcharge her, provided it was accompanied by an appealing tale of approaching paternity. She must have influenced the birth-rate of Florence during her life there as surely as " B. B." influences the book production of England to-day.

All this was based on a single desire for and love of life itself. No annoying tags or joyless humanitarian rationalizations attached to her fecund sympathies. She wanted more children in the world. Once there, she had very definite ideas as to what to do with them; ideas that sprang from an elaborate principle of leaving them alone. A few amazingly simple garments were cut to shelter their limbs from the elements during the first few months and they were fed by the cunning devices nature has evolved and equipped most mothers with. As the months progressed into years, garments of any kind were discarded entirely, save for a few party dresses occasionally donned as a sop to visitors and friends (of whom the house was always full), whose views on the question of bringing up children did not coincide with those of their hostess; in fact, could be called violently opposed. Fruits, nuts, and vegetables were substituted for the natural fare provided during the first months. Meat was banned. No subtle, bacteriological flavour of decay was to taint their palates, not even an egg. This was the regimen by which she herself lived, and the children followed suit. Concessions were made here, as in the matter of dress, to those friends who shared her hospitable board, an excellent Italian cook providing succulent dishes to satisfy the polluted tastes of less enlightened foodists. Difficult to savour a *tournedos* with unconditional enjoyment under her limpid gaze, but accomplishable. Such was her perfected formula of life, and so with easy continence she lived it. She was a musician of no mean degree and sang German *lieder* in a full gracious voice, always a little off key, but always truly.

It was Lily Braggiotti who steered me through the shoals of childbirth; engaged the gentle and wise doctor, the garrulous nurse, the sage, brave midwife; initiated me into mysteries of small long clothes, preposterous bonnets, and archaic cradle; held my hand when I most needed it . . . and found me another nurse when it was discovered that the garrulity of the first one was due to alcoholic stimulus. Her grave young successor deserves a place by herself in the Florentine chronicle. I will find it for her.

Isadore Braggiotti was a different matter entirely. Dedicated to the teaching of singing, imbued with every conservative sophistication his New England blood could bring him, and at the same time pleasantly sensitive to the luxurious laziness flowing through his veins from earlier Oriental sources, he was a complicated symptom of mixed civilizations and humorously aware of it. He adored his wife; and though given to silken raiment, fine linens, spices, sweets and wines, as well as slavish obedience from servants, in deference to her he ate nuts and fruits washed down with water, listened to the unchecked howlings and arrogant demands of his offspring, and viewed their beautiful naked little bodies with perfect equanimity. Only occasionally, under the protection offered by a long dinner-table heaped with flowers in the

8

centre, would he surreptitiously snatch an aromatic squab and quickly swallow a glass of wine, or speculate wittily on the effect his life and family would have on a New England ancestor arriving fresh from Boston. There was no hypocrisy in his attitude; merely a flexibility toward life and a civilized instinct of deference to his wife, to whom these matters were of vast importance. He maintained the same attitude toward his pupils; my husband, Paul Draper, was one of them. We were in Florence for that reason. They came to him from isolated corners of America, pathetically anxious to be prepared in six months, or at the most one year, for the operatic stage. He taught them as long as they stayed and would give " Pupils' Concerts " in the vast galleried music-room of his villa. Any pupil breaking down in the middle of the aria from *Louise,* which all beginners of the female sex modestly insisted upon, or the *Pagliacci* Prologue, which was the equally modest choice of the males, would be waved languorously off the platform and sent up behind the turquoise blue balustrade of the gallery, there to listen while Lily would sing a Brahms' lullaby to a baby yet unborn.

The fruit-filled, nut-nourished, scantily clothed children were always rushing about the villa in glorious confusion. A dancing, violin-playing, singing crew of splendid naked health, who are now scattered to the corners of the earth. Almost impossible to think of them as separate individuals. They were the flowers growing about the feet of those two beautifully unique people.

· · · · · · · ·

Now the parade can go on.

In her haunted villa sat Mabel Dodge. In the nobly arched fourteenth-century courtyard of it ſtood Edwin Dodge, her architeƈt husband, greeting her gueſts and leading them through one perfeƈtly proportioned room after another until they reached an inadequate flight of ſtairs, down which they ſtepped into the less perfeƈtly proportioned room he had added to the villa. Once in the room, the slightly unbalanced scale upon which it was built, the " rich man's red " brocade with which the walls were covered, disappeared in the definite visible atmosphere that Mabel Dodge always creates about her within four walls.

There she sat.

Jacques Blanche was painting her portrait, a pattern of deep red velvets and black feathers, if I remember, but very unrelated to Mabel. Gertrude Stein was writing her portrait in a room near by. There had been an incident of a slow donkey cart expertly avoided by Mabel in a faſt motor on a narrow hill road that day, that had sent Gertrude Stein into a subconscious fury (or was it conscious?) that demanded expression. But that belongs to literary hiſtory. Janet Scudder was defending her lack of objeƈtive in putting up bronze ſtatues of small boys in gardens, saying, " Why, Mabel, I juſt want to put something beautiful in a beautiful place. I don't know why. I have no purpose. I juſt want to put something bea . . ." A tubercular, tailored English woman was explaining that the blue-caped little trained nurse with enormous gold-rimmed speƈtacles whom she had brought

with her had not gone mad, but was juſt having a trance
in the corner. " She sees the spirit of Beethoven tied with
pink ribbons to the piano and is helping him to get free.
Don't mind her," she pleaded, tapping her foot with her
cane.

Mabel did not mind her. She juſt sat there.

Arthur Aƈton, the gilt-edged " rag-and-bone man " of
Florentine antiques, who married a gracious, exquisitely
dressed little American and put her in a perfeƈt villa surrounded by priceless (on second thought, they were not
priceless) furniture and tapeſtries, was, contradiƈtorily
enough, expatiating on the delights of a mechanical piano
recently acquired. Robert de la Condamine, who has
written one important book called *The Upper Garden,*
and is one of England's great aƈtors, was filling the air
with subtly shattering innuendoes. The approach of a
comet was awaited — I forget which; there are not many.
Ghostly manifeſtations in certain gueſt rooms of the villa
were discussed, much to the discomfort of Janet Scudder.

Mabel sat on.

Splendid Mrs. Stanford White was whiſtling and singing at the same time, a feat which fills me with envy to
this day. As to ghosts — " Nonsense! " she exclaimed.
" Roll one pellet of bread under two crossed fingers and
you can swear there are two. So with ghoſts. Uncross your
fingers." Years later, in this very villa, I tried to remember this wholesome advice during a scene in which the
blue-caped little nurse appeared again, playing the chief
rôle. It did not help much.

Janet Scudder was not comforted. Mrs. White's son,

Lawrence White, rushed into the room, bursting with excitement over great pictures he was seeing for the first time.

D'Annunzio was to be brought to tea that day, but the man who was to bring him arrived alone. It seemed that d'Annunzio had taken his first flight in an airplane and had stepped out of it so unpoetically and violently air-sick that the solace offered by bed and bromo-seltzers proved more alluring than the nourishment promised by a new audience, however small.

A gauntly sagging woman with sad grey hair and patient sallow cheeks walked into the room, her arms filled with roses and iris, and said to Mabel Dodge, in a frightened, flat, resigned American voice, " Mabel, I won't pick any more flowers unless you tell Pietro to shut up that white peacock. It is the third time he has attacked me to-day." And with slow, poignant determination she turned and walked out again.

Mabel did not move. She did not have to. She was everywhere. Mabel did not speak. Words were too slow for her. She went quickly into where you lived and found you there, while you were still in the first throes of verbal communication. She was patient. She would wait for you. If you wanted to catch up another time, you would find her there, sitting.

. . . .

I must not let the grave little nurse fall into the abyss of memory. She shall be left in her place. When Lily Braggiotti summoned her from the bosom of an over-populated family in the country to replace the bacchanalian matron who had unwisely guarded my son since birth, she was only fifteen years old. She appeared suddenly in the doorway of the villa which sheltered us, a solemn, silent, underfed little creature, carrying a bundle of clothes under her arm, a shawl pulled across her thin shoulders, and a handkerchief tied under her serious chin. I brought her through the doorway and into the house. I asked her a few questions. Her palpable fright at finding herself in an unknown city, in an unknown house, in the presence of an unknown *signora,* and about to take charge of an unknown baby, made it impossible for her to hear a question, to say nothing of answering one. She nodded her good grave little head occasionally and whispered, " *Si, signora.*" I saw that she was an earnest and utterly trustworthy child and not given to excess, alcoholic or otherwise, so I engaged her. Five minutes later, she was the devoted slave of my son. Five days later, I had revealed the mysteries of the toothbrush with more or less success, fed her, clothed her and begun to love her.

She responded to this treatment with whatever growth her self-contained young nature was capable of, and in five months was a lovely image of protection that stood between my son and all harm. She sang strange minor melodies that were threaded on savage Saracenic wails, as she worked. She ruined all the fine dresses the small son possessed with some biting acid stuff she insisted upon putting in the washtub. She always picked him up when he cried, and would shirk giving him his bath whenever she could manage it, believing it to be "enfeebling." She was, in short, a thoroughly incompetent and endearing little person, whom we loved and trusted.

By an odd combination of circumstances, I possessed an uncut diamond. It had lain in my jewel-box, carefully wrapped in tissue paper, since the day I had sailed from America. The moment came when I was seized with the desire to have it set. I do not like diamonds, but jewellers of Florence are tempting devils, and I knew one who could make it wearable. I took it from the box in luxurious certitude, unrolled the lightly folded paper — and found a miserable brown coffee bean in place of the glistening stone I had myself put there. Now, I repeat, I do not like diamonds, but I like still less a coffee bean in place of one. I hardly dared question myself as to who might have made the ingenious substitution: what with hotels and steamers and trains, any one of a hundred people could have taken it. However, I seemed to remember having looked at it once since settling in the little pink villa.

I consulted Paul. We reluctantly decided that a cowardly search of the servants' quarters was necessary. There were only three servants. There was Rosina: stalwart, handsome young Rosina, engaged to be married, happy, inordinately capable. Her gifts were manifold. She plucked leaves from strange trees that grew in corners of our garden, plunged them in boiling water, left them there until she had brewed a most potent and evil-smelling mixture, then washed my tailored coats and skirts in it, bringing them to me magically renewed. Surely, she

14

could not have taken a hard horrid diamond from her
Signora. Nevertheless, she *was* engaged, and it might
have occurred to her that a diamond would not have
been an inappropriate object to find its way into her
bello's pocket.

There was Eliza: Eliza the unspeakably dirty, the
hysterical, slightly mad Eliza. She was the cook, the
eldest of the three, and we were a bit in awe of her. She
had been known to rush from the kitchen into the waving
cornfield at the back of our small garden, fling herself
on the ground between the sturdy stalks, mingle her sobs
with the rustling of the wind through their leaves, and
wave her angry red-stockinged legs in the air because
I had once suggested — only suggested — that I would
like coffee in the coffee-pot which she nightly filled with
a poisonous mixture of chicory and water. I never suggested it again, for we valued that corn, an unheard-of
luxury in Italy, and had hopefully nurtured it from month
to month. According to the peasants who farmed the
few acres that surrounded us, it had never borne an ear
of corn, but we were taking no risks. No, it could not have
been Eliza. No one who ignored the true worth of coffee
could value a diamond. Still, it *was* a coffee bean which
had lain deceptively in the tissue paper. Could she have
developed a sense of ironic revenge?

And there was Annunziata.

There was only one course open to us. We must search
the rooms of all three. Traitorously, we would send them
out to the *cinematografo* that evening, and have it over
with.

15

After dinner, Paul, falsely kind, told all three to take the evening off, giving them handfuls of money, and fairly pushing them out the door. We waited until they had waved us a final joyous good-night, and then went slowly upstairs and along the corridor to Eliza's room.

We went in. We opened all the drawers of her bureau, and found nothing but a few yellowed undergarments, a red flannel petticoat, a little pile of gaily coloured handkerchiefs, and three half-burnt candles in the corner of the last drawer. Save for the washstand, conspicuously unused, and one chair, there was no furniture in the bare little room, so we hurriedly left it.

We crossed the corridor, and went into the big chamber that Rosina and Annunziata occupied together. We looked through the garments which hung from pegs on the wall, and then went to Rosina's chest of drawers, which was nearest at hand. The top drawer contained a few odd bits of ribbon, some handkerchiefs and the incoherent miscellany which a top drawer usually collects. The next held blouses, her underclothes, gayer and cleaner than Eliza's, and, in one corner, a bundle of crochet-work with which she was garnishing them, one by one, to be ready for her wedding day. The last drawer was filled with several good, strong linen sheets and a pair of blankets, with which she had begun her trousseau. All these we examined carefully, with no result.

There remained but Annunziata's bureau unsearched. The top drawer was much like Rosina's: not so much ribbon, perhaps, and all in better order. The next held underclothes, bare of trimming, very coarse and spotlessly clean. In the laſt drawer lay the white dress she had worn at her first communion, reverently folded, a white prayer-book and a cigar-box. I was pretty well sickened of the business by now, and wanted to leave the cigar-box unopened. I did not care if it was filled with ſtolen diamonds. This invasion of other people's lives muſt cease.

But Paul looked at me ſternly, and said, " We better have it over with," so I pulled myself together and opened the box. It contained an elaborate tin frame holding a piĉture of her siſter in wedding finery, an old silk purse I had given her, with all she had managed to save from her earnings of the paſt months carefully tucked in it; a rosary, a chocolate cigar rolled in silver paper, and, in one corner of the box, a small, — a very small something wrapped in tissue paper. My throat tightened, and with trembling fingers, I begun to unfold it.

So it was Annunziata after all!

I unfolded it further, and my eye caught a glint of gold, — a curve of reddish gold. I spread the paper out on my knee with a gasp of hope, and there lay, carefully tied with a bit of pink ſtring, a short ſtrand of golden hair. . . . At the approach of hot weather, I had commanded Annunziata to crop my son's hair close to his head, and she had tearfully obeyed. Here was the firſt lock of it, preciously saved, and ſtored away amongſt her poor little treasures.

Paul put out his hand, took the box from me, and put it back in the drawer. We crept from the room and down the corridor. Before the door of my room, I paused and said, " Are you going to bed now? "

" No," he answered, looking away from me. " I think I will sit in the garden. They didn't take the keys, you know, and I . . . I . . . I think I would like to stay up and open the door for them."

.   .   .   .

In Florence I met Eleanora Duse.

I could not speak to her. Profoundly moved, I sat and watched her. Every word of Italian or any other language I ever knew deserted me. I feared the sound of my voice would take up space in the room which, if I remained silent, might be filled by hers. She spoke with a voice of wings. She moved with unfathomable rhythm. She permeated the air with the ethereal assurance that she was inhabiting her body, but could leave it if she chose. I did not move. She went away.

The next day I received a note from her asking me to come and see her. I went with fluttering alacrity and waited in the sad enclosed quiet of her living-room until she entered it. Then we talked. Of Beethoven, whose portrait hung in isolated domination of the room. Of Dante and d'Annunzio, she as remote and impersonal about one as the other; it was her valuation of two poets, one dead, the other living. We spoke of the human voice and she brought me into her cell-like bedroom to show me a complicated vapor apparatus for the alleviation of exhausted vocal cords, from which she suffered.

The only other objects of furniture in the room were a narrow stern white bed, a beautifully carved chest of drawers and a bowl of white flowers on the deep window-sill. We talked of my son, then only a few months old. As I left she asked to come and see him and it was arranged.

She came.

Going seldom into the streets, she arrived shrouded in many veils intricately wound and bound about her head and throat. Knots here and pins there gave the impression that seven tiring-women had laboured seven hours with seventy pins to arrange an impenetrable fog of chiffon in which she moved. She asked first to see the baby and I took her into his room. He lay in his crib, all pink and gold, and as she leaned through her dim veiled folds to look at him, he opened his eyes and looked up at her. With one flashing gesture of ineffable grace she flung her arm up to her head and, saying, " So young a thing as he mustn't see such black dreariness as this," she touched the veils with the white magic of her fingers and they unwound, unknotted, unpinned themselves and fell to the floor. Then my son saw her face and she saw his. They both smiled . . . and we went in to tea.

And so the parade dissolves into the background once again. Loeser and Berenson battling with admirable obstinacy for a worthy cause. The Spauldings entertaining with an integrity and generosity no Florentine miasma could abate, as the son fiddled. The Braggiottis making babies and opera-singers in rich confusion. Mabel Dodge sitting while white peacocks and comets threatened the existence of her guests. Annunziata not stealing a diamond. Eleanora Duse pausing in her unending flight to greet my son and leave with me the benediction of her presence. . . . And so to London.

MUSIC AT MIDNIGHT

Steyning

1911

THE LONDON YEARS ARE
more tangible and still retain their three-dimensional
form.

" Luggage, madam? " Pleasant sound. Friendly question. A kind of " If you haven't, I'm so sorry to have
asked. In fact, let it be as if it had never been mentioned,
but if you have, do let me look after it for you " air
about it. Only an English porter at Dover does not laugh
or curse, when, heavily laden with the luggage he has so
politely requested, he hears you cry out to him, " Oh!
the baby's shoes! You know — his old shoes that I tied
on a string for him to play with on the train from Florence. Where are they? He must have them — he'll need
them on the train to London." Only an English porter,
I repeat, does not curse you for being the silly fool you
know you are, but with uncanny divination *finds*
them, adds them ceremoniously to the accumulation
of bags and boxes piled up on his back, and wafts
you gently into a train. . . . Thus we proceeded to
London.

We arrived, baby, old shoes, luggage, Rosina (at the
last moment, Annunziata had been reclaimed by her family), and all, and settled in one of those cherished small
hotels that America so conspicuously lacks, where even

23

the lift seems private and the bread and butter inconceivably thin.

We had decided to come to London in order that Paul Draper could study singing with Raimund von Zur Mühlen, whom Harold Bauer had told us in Florence over a glass of champagne brought in " *una tasse, SUBITO* " at Mrs. Boardman's command, was the greatest teacher of German *lieder* alive. This does not necessarily mean that Braggiotti could not teach, but Paul Draper was not an opera singer. He was a *lieder* singer. So our first day in London we set out to find Zur Mühlen. He had gone to the country. We followed him there and found him in Wiston Old Rectory, a charming house on the estate of Wiston Manor, Steyning, Sussex. English as the house was on the outside, upon crossing the threshold, it became very un-English indeed. Raimund von Zur Mühlen, of Russian extraction, but born a German subject in the Baltic provinces, came to England after thrilling years lived in Germany. He brought with him a fine foreign flavour, a taste for bright yellow walls, Munich Empire furniture, doves, red brocade, and his great genius: all of these could be felt the minute one passed into his house, the last to an awe-inspiring degree. We announced ourselves to the servant who let us in, and asked to see him. She pushed us into a small room, shut the door of it and hurried away. We waited nervously to be sent for. In a few minutes the door opened and a pretty, serious-eyed American girl came through it, with the irritating condescension of one already initiated and, speaking with a great affectation of solemnity said, " I am sorry but I am

24

RAIMUND VON ZUR MÜHLEN FEEDING HIS BELOVED WHITE DOVES, AFTER
FEEDING PAUL DRAPER AND MYSELF STRAWBERRIES AND CREAM

sure the Master cannot see you. He is ill. He is suffering. He cannot see strangers. He must know about you. Write to him and I will try to arrange an appointment. — No, impossible. I am sorry. It is not worth your while to ask him. He suffers. He can see no one. I am *sure* he will not see you."

As she said the last words in hushed tones, a man stood in the doorway behind her. He was tall, with a very beautiful almost-bald head set on broad shoulders, a look of perfectly understood tragedy about his eyes and a smile of deeply understanding humour about his mouth. It was Zur Mühlen himself. One knew it. " So," he said, brushing the prettily chagrined young thing gently away, " So — you have come to see me? And what do you want? Where have you come from? All the way from America! And a little studying in Florence? Ah! yes — America! . . . Would you like some strawberries and cream? Would you like to see the doves? No? It is to learn to sing you have come? Ah . . . yes." . . . Pause, while he looked into Paul Draper, and then, to him: " Well, come in here and sing then." Claiming Paul with a gesture, he turned in the doorway and walked with quick soft steps through a hall and across a threshold into space, Paul at his heels. Seeing them disappear I followed them. I could not stay alone. Once across the threshold we were all three in a large light room; yellow walls, red damask chairs, flowers, pianos, and doors opening on a courtyard of doves. I slipped quietly into one of the red damask chairs and waited. Paul Draper stood in the middle of the floor and waited. Von Zur

Mühlen walked to the open doors and stood with his back to the room, to Paul, to me, to everything but the doves and the courtyard. He waited too. Suddenly he turned with savage ferocity, walked quickly toward his new pupil, and shrieked: " Sing! Stupid idiot. You have come from America to learn how to sing — *begin!*"

Paul Draper began, with no accompaniment and under circumstances as trying as any singer was ever submitted to, you will admit. Yet so exciting was Mühlen's presence and so kind did he somehow manage to seem, that Draper continued. Mühlen listened a minute and then cried: "*Stop!*" Walking over to the doors once again, he said, "Who taught you that 'little studying' in Florence?" He was told. "Clown!" he howled in response, — to the doves. Then, turning into the room once again, he asked, "And before that, in America?" He was told. "Ox!!" he screamed. Then, holding out his arms to Draper, he smiled a radiant smile and summed up as follows: "You are a fine musician. You are an artist. You love German songs. You will know them truly when I truly give them to you, as the men who wrote them gave them to me. You will sing them as Mühlen can no longer sing them. You will sing them as *you* can sing them. But you must work. Come. What is your name again? Paul? Yes, come Paulchen, — and your wife sitting there so strangely, what is her name? Muriel? Yes? Come Paulchen and Muriel, come, we will now eat strawberries and cream and feed the doves. Come along."

So that was how we could not see Mühlen that first day.

A few days later we were installed in the farmhouse of a family named Christmas — baby, old shoes, Rosina *et al.* And there for a summer Paul Draper worked as Mühlen said he must, and things began to happen about his singing as Mühlen said they would.

MUSIC AT MIDNIGHT

London—Holland Street

1911–1912

AND THE SUMMER PASSED. We returned to London when Mühlen did, his enchanted slaves, and he found us a little house opposite his own in Holland Street, which is a short court juſt off Church Street, Kensington. It had belonged to Sir Walter Crane and Dame Crane, his wife, and the monotonously flowering illuſtrations of that benevolent old gentleman were framed into the walls and panels all over the house. No escape. However, it was a charming little house. Uneven floors, a powder room, no butler's pantry, but two of the moſt perfeɛted servants in the world, who were included in the lease and did not mind leaving the roaſt on the top ſtep of the kitchen ſtairs while the soup plates were being removed. Miracles of servants!

While getting the Holland Street house in order, we ſtopped again in our favorite little hotel. There Rosina — awkward, devoted young Italian peasant that she was, away from home for the firſt time, fell ill. Juſt homesickness, she thought. Or perhaps tea and marmalade and sole did not agree with her. I sympathized and cajoled and sent her to Soho for spaghetti and wine, but she came back unsolaced and much sicker. I suggeſted writing to her mother for family news, but this suggeſtion was speedily thrown out. I feared an overwhelming attack of nostalgia might prove fatal to her happiness in London and, as she was a valiant and valuable soul who had adapted herself to the duties of nurse with welcome facility, I dreaded losing her. I besought her to sleep and told her I would call a doctor for her in the morning. I did. He came. . . . Perhaps I had better not go on with the story. Anyway, as she wanted her son to be born in Italy, she went back to Florence shortly after armed with a letter to Lily Braggiotti, who engaged her with passionate immediacy. It seemed her *bello* was at war. Cowardly valour. Ah, well! He returned from the war unscathed and Lily Braggiotti saw to it that Rosina's " homesickness " was assuaged by a home and a husband. The last time I went to Florence she met me at the station with a bunch of red and pink carnations in one hand and her nice clean Italian son, eleven years old, holding on to the other, very happy.

A young Irish angel flew out of a convent and to my aid in the difficulties created by Rosina's departure, mastering the complicated arts of baby's bottles and prams in no time. She moved us into Holland Street, a frail little figure with hair just put up and skirts just let down, and proceeded to manage all of us, including the servants, for the rest of our London years.

To begin them. Attached to the Holland Street house at the back was a large high sky-lighted room, which became the centre of life in that house. We brought into it a Steinway piano, all the sofas we could move in from the rest of the house, unpacked books of written words and written sounds, made room for them by removing countless volumes illustrated by Walter Crane from shelves, and left the rest to the Irish angel and the two miracle maids.

It was October, which can be a dreary month in London. The most important event it heralds is the opening of the concert season. The name of Montague Vert Chester (fantastic name) had been given us as a concert manager of repute and an amateur of music as well. We went to him in search of information concerning the coming season and found him as fantastic as his name. Astute, asthmatic, benevolent, bald-headed and immaculately white-gloved, he mapped out the scene for us, giving us dates of whatever important concerts the season offered. Jacques Thibaud was due soon, and Casals was on his way. He also cautioned us not to miss the début of a young Polish pianist, Arthur Rubinstein, who was at that time practically unknown to European and English audiences. As Paul Draper's musical enthusiasm was not confined to singing and mine was universal, we promised, with high protestations of expectancy, to hear him. As we left Chester's managerial sanctum he made a remark that I was to hear many hundred times during the subsequent years of our friendship. With an arrogance that attempted to conceal a shyness and bridge a difference between manager and musician, he said, " *Moi aussi, je connais la musique. Écoutez!* " and proceeded to hum the opening and closing notes of an octave, repeating it many times, " Tum, *ta* ta tum, *ta* ta tum — *taaaa tummmm* . . ." adding proudly, " Beethoven." This he would do on the slightest pretext, in any key, on any occasion, and though the composer's name sometimes varied, the theme remained the same. After all, he was often right. Apart from this he really possessed a very fair knowledge of music, an unqueſtionably sincere love for it and almost unfailing taſte. He merely wished to participate in the aċtive performance of music as diſtinguished from the passive rôle of appreciating it and so his little futile song of " Tum, *ta* ta tum, *ta* ta tum — *taaa tummmm* . . ." which transformed him for a brief moment into a great conduċtor, a virtuoso of the violin, a maſter singer of oratorio, or a thrilling pianiſt, as the moment moved.

With his little melody in our ears, we rushed back to Holland Street, and after such tea and bread and butter as only those two miracle maids could prepare, and such a delightful hour with our son as only the Irish angel could ensure, we began to plot. If Jacques Thibaud was coming to London from France to play on his violin and Pablo Casals was arriving from Spain to play on his cello, and Arthur Rubinſtein hurrying from Poland to play on his piano, why could not they all play together at one time, and in one place, the one place being the large high room in which we sat? We telephoned Montague Vert Cheſter in great excitement, and, though the prospeċt ſtartled him, his mouth watered with delight at the idea (you could hear it water) as he said: " Don't be in such a hurry. It's weeks or months before they'll be here and they mightn't like it and, — oh! you Americans are always in such a hurry. Hold on a bit. How are you going to manage it? "

" Why, we were just going to ask them, that's all."

" Well, hold on a bit! "

We held on a bit and then a few weeks later the telephone rang and Montague Vert Chester was at the other end. " That Pole I spoke of to you, Arthur Rubinstein, you remember? Well, he is in London. Going to be here for the season. Shall I bring him to dinner? "

" Yes," I snapped, " to-night."

" There you are. Always in such a hurry. Very well, I'll bring him to-night," and he hung up.

So he brought him.

When Rubinstein entered the room it became suddenly smaller. He had a young, short body and broad shoulders, from which long arms ended in the most powerfully sensitive hands I have ever seen. Above those shoulders appeared an ageless, grotesquely ugly face at the prow of a beautiful head. This head was topped with a crop of gracelessly crimped dun-blond hair that sprang aggressively from a high concentrated forehead. Eyes pale with intensity seemed more like hieroglyphics of intelligence than eyes in a face and a sombre Semitic nose carved with chastening Polish delicacy supported them. Pale firmly-full lips smiled with nervous sadness over strange teeth, and only the chin was allowed to rest a little from the forward-moving pace of his vitality. It afforded a slight pause in the breathless race to take in the rest. The next minute you realized that its backward movement was controlled with a fierceness that could defeat a Napoleon. I wonder if all really great men have had the firm prominence so generally accorded this feature? When I think of the strong chins I have known, I doubt it. Be that as it may, Arthur Rubinstein entered the room, Montague Vert Chester puffing with showmanship behind him.

We dined. That is all that can be said for it. It was difficult to converse with this dynamo: words withered in the blast. We just dined, four of us. Afterward we went into the large high room and that nervous thing began in all of us, at any rate three of us, as to whether or not this pianist was going to play without being asked or whether he *would* play if asked. Even Chester began to talk politics with me, and that needed harsh treatment. Finally I turned to Rubinstein desperately, and said: " If you play the way you *are,* please begin."

So with beautiful Polish courtesy, he rose, bowed, thanked me, and went to the piano. He sat down and plunged at once into the Hammer Klavier sonata of Beethoven. This work had always been one of my pet aversions and a subject of acrid intimate debate with my husband. His worship of that isolated figure of impassioned serenity would brook no criticism of any single note written by his hand, not even the Hammer Klavier, and only my oft repeated but never fulfilled threat of playing it could terminate the recurrent debates. I still protest that it can be very boring. In fact, in my ignorance, I conceived of it as never being anything else. It was a composition I liked to discuss, to read, to complain about, but not to hear, NO, definitely *not* to hear. Well, I take it all back. I only regret that I am deprived of one of my cherished resistances to the nobility that is

Beethoven. I still cling sourly to a few of the violin sonatas, the first and third symphony (I have a weakness
for the second) and the song *An die Ferne Geliebte*. It
lasts thirteen minutes by the clock. I have timed it often.
I do not like to listen to a singing voice that long at a
stretch. I just do not like it. Rubinstein played the
Hammer Klavier sonata that night as it was meant to be
played and as it must have been essentially conceived. It
became a work of monumental splendour through his
fingers. Such was the young Polish pianist in 1911. He is
now one of the great pianists of his time. Busoni is dead.

After playing he talked, principally of his beloved
friend Karol Sczymanowski, who was writing great
works in Poland and who wanted to come to England.
One symphony had already been conducted by Fitelberg
in Vienna and the few who know the work of a true
genius as soon as they hear it were valiantly acclaiming
him against less fortunate critics. He had also written
songs and Rubinstein wanted Draper to sing them. He
would come again very soon and bring them. They were a
little difficult perhaps, yes, but he would play them himself to Zur Mühlen and together the three would work
them out. And so he left, Chester trotting ponderously
behind him, smoothing his white gloves and warbling
asthmatically his " Tum *ta* ta tum " to the midnight
air. This time, for instance, he was right.

. . . .

The next excitement was the announcement of
Jacques Thibaud's concert. We went. The true musicianship of this fine artist, the style and dexterity with

37

which he interprets it, puts him in the highest rank of violinists. When he is at the top of his form, few can equal him. Uneven, mercurial, melancholy, cynical, he often disappoints and falls far short of his capacities. He was at the top of his form that night, and — nothing could stop us, not even Chester — Paul and I went " behind " to the artists' room after the concert and told him so, adding that we were going to take him back to a large high room for supper and perhaps . . . At this juncture Chester appeared, breathless and apprehensive, but it was too late. He explained to his professional charge that we were two music-mad Americans, not dangerous, but, well — the damage was done, and if M. Thibaud was not too fatigued, etc., etc., etc. . . . So back we went to Holland Street. Others followed us out of the air and we found Baroness von Hutten and Henry Ainley awaiting us on the doorstep. Now, fascinating as Jacques Thibaud is and anxious as I am to get him across the threshold and into the house so you can hear and see a little more of him, I must pause a moment on that doorstep to present Baroness von Hutten.

A little heavily tall, an exquisitely shaped head with Americanized Greek features, a conspicuously well-bred way of carrying it, slim arms and slimmer fingers, long slender feet, humorous green-brown eyes, and darkly burning red hair. (I should be a passport inspector.) Born, if I remember, in Pennsylvania, she had married a German Baron, borne him a child or two, and then begun to commute to England. Her books, *Pam* and

Pam Decides, charming of their kind, had been read with gay appreciation in London, and her rare beauty did the rest. She was received everywhere for a brief and gala period. A spectacular and romantic episode with one of England's great journalists only added to the lustre of her career and people tolerantly commented, " Well — Pam decided," and asked her to dine. And then somehow it became a little cumbersome . . . that commuting to Germany. Her Baron, after all, where was he? A little unchivalrous of her perhaps, or possibly she became a trifle burdensomely garrulous. Ladies do, when indiscretion achieves a degree of success that renders reticence unnecessary to its indulgence. In any case, when she turned her green-brown eyes from the romantic journalist to focus them on the very beautiful English actor Henry Ainley, and it began all over again, London found the exercise of tolerance as a habit less entertaining than as a function of amused benevolence, and began to show it. Bless them, they were right. In spite of her previously catalogued charms and talents, she could be a very trying woman in the long run, particularly when surrounding herself with all the time-honored conventions of unconventional relationships. Up to that night on the doorstep it had been a short run. She had a gift for companionship and could eat plover's eggs and pig's feet at the Ritz with you on just the day when plover's eggs and anything else would have driven you mad, and yet, plover's eggs you must eat. That is companionship. But she could drink port alone, and that made it tiresome, because she got so controversial. She and Henry Ainley had been drinking port together that night, so they were merely delightfully conversational, and in they came with us.

This brings us back to Thibaud. His slender body moved with a quick alertness which invaded his somewhat surprisingly massive head, constantly flung back to throw his heavily falling black hair from his eyes. A face that could go dead and come alive in swift succession was ever contradicting itself: a heavy cynicism could drag his mouth and eyes down, but a sudden childlike smile could pull it up again. Everything about him intelligent — intelligent to the point of indifference until he took up his violin. Then intelligence became the spirited ally of a white incandescent heat in which his true music-consciousness was bathed; from the subtle fusing of both emerged, at times, the finest fiddling I have heard. Not always. His very qualities occasionally defeated him, exhausted him. He could be stubbornly lazy, or carried away by a kind of nervous clowning of mind and body, executed with agility.

. . . .

Harold Bauer, whose wise enthusiasms, information and advices about von Zur Mühlen had confirmed Paul Draper's wavering choice of singing-masters and sent us to London, came to Holland Street that night too, and together he and Thibaud played one of the Brahms violin sonatas, the one in A Major, if I remember. The grave beauty and infinite gradations of Bauer's playing are never more happily demonstrated than when it supports, penetrates and completes the music of other instruments in ensemble performances. He subdues that

roar which, when he is playing alone, sometimes becomes
a mere heavy shake of soft obstructing sound, pouring
out under his left hand and up from his pedalling feet
into the lower register of a piano — subdues it and builds
it into the distinguishable and cumulative volumes of
vibration that one needs to hear in great climaxes. His
very listening to other qualities of sound than those he
produces on the piano makes him hear himself more
clearly. Some of the most inspired performances of works
written for chamber music with piano, have been when
he was seated at that instrument. Possibly it is due to the
fact that he began his musical education with the study
of violin and all its literature, graduating from the Royal
College of London a full-fledged violinist with honours,
before he dedicated his musical gifts to the piano.

His performance that night with Thibaud was superb.
Even Baroness von Hutten obeyed the imperative demand for silence that I issued, a demand based on the
only condition I ever imposed upon those unforgettable
occasions, which was that no one who did not make
music or love it could be there. The limitless generosity of
those great artists who filled my house and heart and ears
and mind with the pure golden stream of their accom-
plishment was too rare a gift to be endangered by an im-
perfectly grateful acceptance. It was all I could offer in
return. Paul Draper could give of his unique art, which
grew to full maturity through the auspicious ritual of
Zur Mühlen's teaching and was already of a musical integrity and taste that sprang from deep roots. He sang that
night and Bauer played the piano for him. (I was too ter-

rified at the prospect.) More Brahms. For me there can never be enough.

Chester was in an *extase*. When we went in to supper he pulled off his white gloves, or rather, removed them — he never *pulled* them off, and fell upon all the pink food he could see and devoured it. He had a great fondness for pink food. I leave it to those who are interested to find out why. I only know that pink food, my son, and music were his three weaknesses during the time I knew him. I found at least two of them the most endearing ones in the world; the third shone in their reflected glory, and I racked all London for pink and pinker food as suppers progressed. It had no relation to taste; a mousse of ham or a raspberry fool (divine English sweet that it is!) were all the same to him, provided they were pink. One got terribly fond of Chester.

Mrs. Napier was there that night, she to whom, as " the wittiest woman in India," Kipling had dedicated his *Plain Tales from the Hills*. Small, very erect, brilliant blue eyes that saw everything, vitally waving grey hair, parted demurely in the middle, and a tongue that told what her alert mind and unfailing humour selected from it. I had met her in Florence at Mabel Dodge's and had there begun a friendship which the London years nourished, proving her increasingly stimulating and inexhaustibly kind. She was of Irish and English blood, with all that that double inheritance can bring to life, and had a distinguished soldier brother, General Munro, who in years that followed covered himself with glory in his chosen profession. At supper she entered into a pretty

42

passage of arms with the beautiful Baroness, who ill-
advisedly questioned her as to why the previous cordiality shown her by some mutual friend had been so
gradually but firmly withdrawn. Mrs. Napier answered
her with an exquisite irony, a nimble avoidance of bru-
tality and unerring flashes of truth expressed with an
ultimate choice of words which left me breathless. I give
the outline of her technique rather than the actual conversation, as in the cold path of time it might lie an unneces-
sarily painful pebble to the bravely walking feet of the
belated Baroness who is, after all, a rather splendid structure of courage, prodigality, and incurable sentimen-
tality. I wish she would write another book in which the
house " smelled of potatoes and three o'clock in the
afternoon," — an apt sense-imagery.

. . . .

And so it began, that golden era of life in London,
and continued until 1914–15, years that melted most
golden things into lead with a hideous reversal of the
highest aims of alchemy.

The nucleus formed by Rubinstein, Thibaud, Bauer,
and Draper proved magnetic. Casals was scheduled for
a concert at Wigmore Hall, and Chester, completely
pacified by now and becoming gradually accustomed to
" going so fast," was agreed that Casals should come to
Holland Street. I wrote him a note. Rumours having already reached him to the effect that it was for music we
asked him, not for lionizing, he came, bringing his
cello with him. We had been to his concert and, as it
was my first hearing of what I believe to be a great inter-

pretive musical genius, it was an event. I had watched his face, his body, his fingers as he played, and marvelled at the exclusive dedication of himself to his cello. Short, almost completely bald, his small body was somehow indefinably enlarged by the significance of his head, by his arrogant impersonality and smouldering compactness of movement. Holding the cello between his knees, he would turn his head slightly away over his right shoulder and, meeting himself alone in some far place that lay beyond the mechanism of his instrument and the sure dexterity with which he touched it, he listened with unyielding curiosity to the music that issued from it. The sound structure that he builds, the austere discipline with which he builds it and the poignant beauty of tone that pervades it, are unique. He transcends his medium and, though you approach the experience of hearing him with all the functions that music brings into use, the experience itself remains independent of them.

Music is to me the symbol by which one may invade the enchanted province of nothing and find one's way. By following its directions, I feel that in some inexplicable way one perceives lines upon which the universe is coördinated. All other arts are more or less dimensionally confined, the boundaries clearly marked out and all-contained. Music forces you to recognize that there is more beyond, to which we have lost the key. Its synthesis of higher mathematics (the most 'mystic' science of all) and highest emotion is the closest approximation of reason with intuition that any art offers. Casals knows it. He does not create it, but he knows it. No one cre-

44

ates it. One is more or less powerfully conscious of it. This is a long introduction to him but I present him as I sensed him when he came into the Holland Street studio, bearing his cello carefully before him.

He was happy to find Thibaud and Bauer and, after a long glass of milk and a long cigar, his choice of refreshment from the fatigue of playing, he was anxious to play again. I have noticed with musical artists that a concert acts as a preliminary stimulus, and that granted the conditions, they can go on playing until dawn. Knowing that the only reason people are listening is because they desire it, and that the taste and musical knowledge of fellow-players enable them to give and take every phrase at full value, brings a pleasure to such spontaneous exercise of their gifts which is often lacking in professional performances. They decided on the Beethoven piano trio in D Major and proceeded to play it, Bauer at the piano, Thibaud violining, and Casals playing his beloved instrument. The brilliant opening movement, the moving theme of the second, the vigour of the last, played by those three men, sing in my ears as I write. Casals, by now really aroused, followed the Beethoven trio with the sixth Bach suite, unaccompanied. The flawless organic growth of this work from the first note to the last was presented with all the conviction this artist could bring to it. After that no one could ask for more. Even for the house in Holland Street, the evening had been a good one.

. . . .

It was soon evident that reinforcements were needed, if those artists already at home in Holland Street were going to be able to play as much chamber music as they wished. We held counsel, and the need was answered. Casals brought to us one Rubio, a friend of his and a very good cellist. To be a friend of Casals, and a good cellist to boot, was enough to have endeared him to us, but the man was so lovable a person in himself that he won an enduring affection from every one who came in contact with him. He was a Spaniard and looked like a seventeenth-century Spanish painter's idea of a gentle God with a flowing beard, reclining easily on billowy clouds in a very solid heaven. He had skin like gold-and-brown parchment, eyes of deeper brown velvet that would trust a murderer, and black-grey-white hair growing in kindly profusion on his head and chin. He spoke a mixture of Spanish, French, Italian and English, made more than linguistically intelligible by the large emphatic gestures that accompanied it, indeed, often outstripped it. A love of music, an adoration of God and Pablo Casals, and a cherished delusion in the matter of knowledge concerning pictures were the dominant elements of his character. The walls of his modest room in King's Road were lined with " masterpieces." In his eyes this water-colour was unquestionably a Sargent, executed in such haste that there was not even time for him to affix his signature; these fresh tones and abundant flesh could have been conceived by none other than Rubens himself; while that small wooden panel flaked with gold and a flight of white was unmistakably Fra Angelico. Dear lamb, to be so fleeced! The proud pleasure they afforded him was of greater value than most collectors receive from their au-

thentic canvases and therefore not to be regretted save
from the angle of expenditure. It was heart-breaking to
think of this dear trusting man diminishing his small
horde of earnings in proportionate ratio to his increasing
years. He was a brave cellist, occasionally rising to heights
by the purity of tone he produced and the unerring musical rhythm which formed every phrase. Always eager, his
experience and knowledge of chamber music made him
of irreplaceable value on these evenings which were now
becoming an integral part of life in Holland Street. I hope
he is still alive. He made a second cellist for sextets and
often first cellist in duets and trios. He always introduced
Casals with a beaming smile as " Pablissimo," a superla-
tive which needed no explanation.

Harold Bauer told of his sister Gertrude, who, it seems,
played an excellent viola. She joined our forces and was
one of the most untiring and loyal members of it. She
would arrive on time, grimly cheerful, unpack her viola
with as tender a gesture as she was capable of, and sitting
on her rightful chair of the four or six that were grouped
with music-stands in front of them, would open the music
written for her instrument and study it, sometimes with
viola, sometimes silently to herself. Then, while the rest
of the musicians took their seats and found their parts,
she would sit back and rest a minute before the work
began. Once in her stride, she would never stop. The
skies could fall, the walls crash in, G strings could snap,
her brother drop dead at the piano, but she would go on
unswervingly to the end of the movement. Well trained
as Harold Bauer's sister inevitably would be, thoroughly

music-read and knowing her way through almoſt every work, she had a devotion to music that compensated for her complete lack of any sensuous beauty of tone. Her ſturdy bowing and accurate tempi never failed her. She was never hurt if another viola player appeared on the scene, always ready to ſtay in her chair playing until dawn, or give it up at any moment and liſten absorbedly for the reſt of the evening. Eventually we could not do without her.

· · · · · · · ·

Emerson Whithorne made his appearance that year. His skilful, saturnine, sulkily beautiful face was a ſtill flag of silence for many evenings. And then one night he spoke.

" Why so damned much Beethoven? " he exploded.

" Because I have heard enough Chopin," I explained.

Then he smiled. The ſtill flag of his face waved a little and he began to talk, exceedingly well, of music ancient and modern, with a nervous surge of excitement that flowed all about the latter and a certain ſterile reluctance running through his admiration of the former. No wonder! He was writing music himself after years of concentrated ſtudy with a maſter of orcheſtration. He was at that time inveſtigating with the electric virtuosity that characterizes his work to-day, the subtle and complex temptations of rhythm that the development of sound through modern orcheſtration has put before composers in this firſt part of the twentieth century. He had written several songs and was working on a ſtring quartet and symphonic work for orcheſtra. We led him to the piano and he played some of his songs, singing the melody in one of those unhuman voices with which, for some obscure reason, all composers are endowed. However their voices may vary, in one respect they are unchangingly the same, and that is in respect to strangeness. The voice of a composer is the *strangest* sound in the world. If you know one, ask him to sing. Ask him to " hum the part through," if it is a work for solo instrument. Just ask him. . . . However, in spite of this sound, Whithorne's songs were deft rhythmic dissonances of unquestionable musical worth. I remember particularly the lovely lunatic cadences of *Delua,* written to Fiona McLeod's magic poem of that name. He promised to bring the quartet when finished for a trial performance, and I promised not to discuss Beethoven for one whole evening unless the B Flat posthumous quartet was mentioned, or the Scherzi of the Sixth and Ninth Symphonies were attacked.

He spoke of his wife Leginska who, with their child, was on her way to London from Vienna, and of her brilliant gifts as a pianist. When she arrived, he would bring her to Holland Street, and we should hear for ourselves. He did bring her shortly after. Her head, that was large in proportion to the tiny body that supported it, wore a face of furtive dissipations, pools of eyes lying shadowed under shags of hair. Diabolically strong small fingers sprang out of hands that hung inertly from slight shoulders. She spoke little, but was eager to play. No first-rate artist that I have known is ever loath to. She sat down and tore out of the piano with a dizzy clarity of technique

49

the Brahms Paganini variations. She spoke of composing
(not of conducting!) and outlined a strange map of musical aberrations she was preparing. The few snatches
of it that I remember sounded gauchely vicious, and I
longed for her to play again. She, graciously enough, proceeded to some Debussy, which she played with dazzling
intelligence. It was a fine talent in those days.

Henry Ainley was fascinated by her. They both came
from Yorkshire I believe and he used to address her as
Ethel Leggins, which amused her vastly. Ainley was
incredibly beautiful and had a voice that vibrated in your
spine and echoed on the roof of your mouth. It was his
beauty and his voice that procured for him his first serious
part on the London stage. He had been playing in the
provinces and some alert chance person had heard him
and snatched him to London to play in a forthcoming
production of *Paolo and Francesca*. He stoutly averred
that he had not the slightest idea at any time during the
performance of what any word in it meant, that he carried it through by sheer instinct for rhythm, to a success
that was a greater surprise to him than to anyone else
concerned. Since that time his work on the English stage
has brought him authority and prestige. A natural intelligence and emotional intensity, in addition to the voice,
have done it for him. His stressful scenes with the
Baroness were somehow delightful. They would wrangle
with the bitterness that so often stamps such situations,
but dear Ainley could not maintain for long the high
pitch of fictitious tragedy that Baroness von Hutten at
times imposed. His natural sweetness and simple desire

to be happy, or at least comfortable, would gain the upper hand and he would break down with an engaging " Now, Bess, be a dear and I'll recite the *Bells of Breedon* to you and then we'll go have a pork pie and some ale, but let's not discuss whether the servants should call you ' your ladyship ' or not any longer. I will call you ' your ladyship ' if you insist, though I think Betsy Riggs has a much nicer sound, but let's not have any more back-chat about it." Spoken in anyone else's voice this speech would be a justifiable cause for murder, but in his . . . Well, I have heard him recite *Bells of Breedon* at least a score of times and never without effect. He adored her and they were a beautiful brace of human beings to look at.

One night Paul and I came home from a *lieder* concert of Julia Culp's and stopped in to tell Mühlen of it, who went rarely to concerts but insisted upon an accurate reporting of those in which he was interested. We found him in his little upstairs sitting-room wrapped in shawls, suffering from an attack of neuritis which was torturing him. Through moans of pain he questioned us, and over groans of sympathy we answered him. In the middle of this the bell rang downstairs and a servant came up to announce " Baroness von Hutten and Mr. Ainley to see you, sir."

" I can't see them. I won't see them. Tell them to go away," he called out irascibly in tones that could have been heard across the street.

The servant scurried out and down to translate the message as politely as possible to the wilfully romantic pair below. That booming *Bells of Breedon* voice of Ainley's came echoing through the street door and up the stairway, saying these words, "Tell him I heard him and I won't go away. Her ladyship, Baroness von Hutten " [no Betsy Riggs this time,] "and I will wait until he does see us," accompanied by a sound of determined feet crossing the threshold into the downstairs hall.

This was too much for Mühlen. With a bound he left his chair, shawls and all, and flew out into the upper hall like a wounded animal, trailing the shawls behind him. Leaning over the stair rail he commanded: " Go out of my house, I tell you! Go out of my house!! I will not see you. I am suffering. Go *out* of my house!!! " He, the most hospitable and generous of hosts, was driven to this.

Ainley's " B. of B." voice came raging up: "I will *not* go. Not even God can refuse to see me, once I am in His House."

" God perhaps cannot, but Mühlen *can!* " he shouted down in awful tones.

There was a silence. Footsteps recrossed the threshold. A door closed. Mühlen came back into the little sitting-room, crouched into his chair, pulled the shawls about him once more, and with the smile of an angel, said: " And now, my Paulchen, tell me, at what tempo did she take the *Sapphische Ode?* They *will* sing it too slow, these women."

He was really the kindest of men. These bursts of rage were rare and just. Nervous and often in severe pain from the hideous gnawings of his malady, he would work himself up to an explosion, but, except in such cases as the above, there was always a discernible twinkle in his eye. A fine Rabelaisian flavour permeated his conversation, and I regret that much of it cannot be recorded here. His wit was inimitable. His attitude toward his pupils was a mixture of tenderness, hopeful patience and violently ſtimulating criticism. To sit through a lesson was an unforgettable experience. The care with which he trained whatever accompaniſt happened to be employed thus privilegedly was an education in itself, as Victor Beigel can atteſt, or should. Merciless nicknames filled the air. One admirable young man, slightly over two hundred pounds in weight and much above the average in shyness, was always addressed as " Fatty." Mühlen would ſtop a lesson to berate " Fatty " on the interpretation of some phrase and then, when the poor boy was on the verge of tears, Mühlen would cross over to him, pat him on the shoulder and say very lovingly: " There now, Fatty *darling,* only because you *can* play it so well do I scold you. With fools I am always pleasant. Now run along and take a good . . ." But, alas! I cannot quote here the sentence in full. Be that as it may, by the time " Fatty " returned to the room a few minutes later, he was, to be sure, much relieved and the lesson could continue.

On very rare occasions he left his house to come and dine with us. One of these was to take issue with Robin Legge, the famous music critic of the London *Times,* on certain written opinions which that learned gentleman had expressed. Chief amongſt them was again the question of the tempo in which an artiſt had sung *Sapphische*

Ode, which had seemed to Legge too fast. The discussion waxed furious until Mühlen worked himself up into one of those splendid outbursts, culminating in, " Robin *darling,* you are a fool. I know these songs. I have been the midwife at the birth of these songs. With the poet who wrote *Sapphische Ode,* I lived in Munich when Brahms came running into the room with the ink with which he had written that song still wet on the page. I tell you, he wrote it to be sung fast. Bitches they are, these women who vomit it slowly into the audience's faces. Fast it should be flung to the feet of angels. I tell you, I *know* these songs."

He did, as no one else now living could know them. Brahms was his friend. Clara Schumann was his friend and gave him all that memory could supply of knowledge concerning every note her husband wrote. Apart from his circle of musical intimates, his worldly and political contacts were innumerable. Bismarck had been his friend, and to receive from him tales of that stormy, ill-fated genius and his Emperor, was an exciting event. During the winter he would go to his house in Steyning for a few days at the end of the week as often as pupils and pains would allow. He seldom crossed the street and entered our house unless sure of finding us alone. It was becoming increasingly difficult for him to be happy in the midst of people who were not his intimate friends, and though he would listen eagerly to tales of the music that was played and the musicians who played it, he could not make the effort of joining in it. Early in the spring he moved to his beloved Steyning. Casals went off to Spain,

Rubinstein disappeared into pastoral regions of Poland. Thibaud fulfilled his last London engagement, and Bauer headed toward America. This thinning of the ranks brought the thrilling season of music to rest and so, following Mühlen to Steyning, we left the little house in Holland Street folded in the stilled vibrations of sound which had filled it. May it never be quite empty of them. We did not live there again.

MUSIC AT MIDNIGHT

Steyning
1912

THE FAMILY CHRISTMAS OF
Steyning did not shelter us that summer; I think the combination of Americans and a baby and singing, to say
nothing of Rosina, had proved too much for them the
previous year. In any case they very courteously but firmly
refused. I was disappointed, for they were a bewildering
family. I must shirk them in this narrative, as they are
a book by themselves and could not be confined within
these casual pages, though the governess attendant upon
the innumerable progeny tempts me. She felt she had a
great musical bond with Draper, for she too admired
Brahms, it seemed; in fact, she had gone to London to
hear him sing in 1904 or thereabouts! I was too startled
upon first hearing this to pursue it but, gathering composure, I questioned her a few days later and received
the same answer. Yes. She had heard him sing in London
in 1904. I confessed that I did not know he ever sang, that
I had not heard he was in London in 1904, in fact, had
always believed that he had departed a world grown too
small for him in 1897. " Ah! no. He sang, oh! so beautifully — such lovely songs. No one ever sang like Brahm."
So that was it. A gentleman by the name of Brahm or
perhaps just Bram, who doubtless sang very well, had
given a concert in London in 1904 and this poor faded

59

young lady had heard him and clung to it through all succeeding years as a great musical experience. I would try to put her right, as gently and tactfully as possible without destroying her retrospective pleasure. She understood, oh, yes, quite — it might be confusing to one who did not know, but Brahms, when he sang in London in 1904 just dropped the *s* off his name, that's all. You can see how seductive that family could be to my errant pen, which, if ever trained, may set to work in their behalf. Forgive the digression.

By an appropriate verbal progression from the family Christmas, we found ourselves at Dove's Farm. The family was less absorbing, but pleasanter. It consisted of one tidy little widow who looked after us and did something uncannily successful with lemon, veal and cream, an achievement I have laboured unsuccessfully to rediscover in cooks seen and unseen ever since, but in vain. Either I do not describe it very well, or it was her particular and exclusive mission in life; or perhaps it was all a dream. In any case, it was a bright spot in the otherwise monotonous procession of roast beef, roast lamb and — when I could shoot one (which was about one out of every thirty-seven) — a jugged hare. No summer is long enough to eat one hare shot out of thirty-seven very often unless you do nothing else but shoot them. And I did. I walked through the woods to von Zur Mühlen's house every day, to listen to the extraordinary revelation of song his teaching contained and watch the fascinating effect of it on Paul's art. Mühlen loved him and lavished the wealth of his vast knowledge and experience on the further development of what he considered a great talent. It was as if he felt himself going out of life and was reverently anxious to find some worthy repository in which to leave his precious burden of truth about the songs of Schubert, Schumann and Brahms. Those three composers were his gods. He did not wish to leave their altars unattended, and the summer was given over to them.

MUSIC AT MIDNIGHT

London—19 and 19A Edith Grove
1912–1913

It was during this summer that we decided to find another London house. The studio in Holland Street was not really large enough or high enough for eight instruments and we had discovered that Thibaud's favourite relaxation was to play first violin in the Mendelssohn octet. Anyway, these Walter Crane flowers had gotten on my nerves. So we went up to London on a hot Friday to hunt for one and as almost every house in London is livable, we did not have to hunt long. Being bound by no conventions as to locality — two mad young Americans in London could go where they liked — we found two houses, one back of the other, in Edith Grove.

Edith Grove! The two words are a country to me as I write them to-day, and in that country Number 19 is the Capital. At 19 and 19A Edith Grove were two houses, and we took them. There had been a Maud Grove and a Clara, due to the paternal sentiment of a previous land-holder toward his three daughters, amongst whom he had doubtless divided the property and stamped it with their dear silly names. Maud and Clara Grove had given way to less fragile designations, but Edith Grove miraculously remained. Moving up from Steyning earlier than Mühlen, we went to our beloved hotel for a brief interval while I did some house-wrecking.

By pulling out all the insides of 19A, I made out of a house a room big enough for the Mendelssohn octet. I left nothing but the brick walls, which I pierced with windows and a fireplace, and the roof of the house, in which I put a skylight and across which I stretched iron rods for support. By knocking a hole in one wall, I pushed a staircase through from 19A to 19, taking down a solid little stone fence that had separated them. And then we moved in. We traitorously seduced the miracle maids away from their former employers, and they moved in with us. The Irish angel had never left our side. All was well.

Arthur Rubinstein, returned to London for the season, found us a matchless Bechstein piano. A Kien Lung screen unfolded itself on one side of the room and a huge sofa was built to fit another side. Plenty of small chairs for the players and plenty of big ones for the listeners were chosen: floor cushions, of a size that made it possible for a half dozen people to sit, or one tired artist to sleep if he arrived exhausted from a performance, were piled high in the corners of the room. Amazing how a pianist could sleep while someone sang, or how a violinist could dream during a suite for cello.

Musicians of the Holland Street era were flocking back to London and we planned our welcoming party in Edith Grove to coincide with Thibaud's first concert engagement. I was determined that he should have his Mendelssohn octet. He did. Rubinstein had brought the distin-

66

guished violinist, Paul Kochanski, back with him from Poland and brought him to Edith Grove, an act for which I am forever in his debt. Several additions to the musical ranks were made that night. Friends brought more friends, as the echoes of the music made in Holland Street the year before had spread far and wide, and all musicians like to play.

The first fire was burning in the fireplace of 19A. Huge candles were lighted in every dim corner of the room. Small powerful electric bulbs were snapped into use over the music-stands and on them the parts of the Mendelssohn octet were opened at page 1.

Thibaud and Kochanski played first violins, Persinger and Morales second, Harold Bauer's sister loyally acquitted herself of the responsibility of second viola to Lionel Tertis' first, May Mukle and the saintly Rubio assuming the delightful duties of the two cellists.

Thibaud was in a frenzy of delight and high spirits and brought to the octet a dignity and brilliance for which its composer should thank him if ever the uncertainties of time and place involved allow. Excited by the beauty of performance and the thrilled listening contained within those brick walls, everybody wanted to play everything, — to make music and more music forever. This want, born that night of the first music-making in Edith Grove, did not die. It grew in that place to greater strength than walls of brick and burned more brightly hot than wood.

· · · · · · · ·

From that first night hardly a week passed without music at Edith Grove. Some new work to be heard or some newly arrived musician to be welcomed brought us together at a moment's notice.

If, on a night when an artist was giving a concert with orchestra, to be followed by an evening in 19A, we found ourselves faced with a possible vacancy in the personnel necessary to the desired performance of any particular work, our methods were simple. They consisted merely in accosting, on our trips back stage to the artists' rooms, whatever member of the disbanding orchestra we found possessed of the instrument necessary to fill the vacancy and asking him if he would like to come back to Edith Grove and play some chamber music. To their eternal honour be it said that not one ever refused. To the contrary, I have never known a professional musician who was not willing and, indeed, eager to play with the great artists of their chosen profession. Many's the bassoon and French horn we have deterred from their homeward path in the name of music. Many's the double-bass who has overcome the almost insurmountable difficulties engendered by the proportions of his instrument in order to spend an hour or two or three or five in delighted wayfaring through octets and small orchestral works. Occasionally one would fall by the wayside in despair, as witness the following, sad letter from the faithful Victor Watson:

2, Moyser Road
Streatham, S. W.
20. 4.

Dear MRS. DRAPER,

         I was very sorry indeed to disappoint you the other evening, but muſt ask you to believe that I did all in my power to keep the engagement. I could not get a porter to carry my bass, so after the evening's engagement, I went myself to Queen's Hall. I succeeded in obtaining a taxi after waiting twenty minutes for one, but the cabman refused to open the top for my inſtrument to be got in. On account of the heavy rain, I had to give it up as impossible. Press of business and a removal to above address have prevented me writing before, for which I tender my sincere apologies.

         I remain,

         Yours sincerely,

         VICTOR A. WATSON **(M. H.)**

P. S. Mr. Watson is indisposed.

Victor Watson was an indomitable soul and this was his one misfortune. He never failed us again and often filled the roof of 19A with the splendid dark surge of controlled sound that he could bring forth from his double-bass. His firſt ill-fated adventure caused him to take every possible precaution thereafter and I cannot hold it againſt him that his habit of sending his huge bass cello on hours before him when circumſtance allowed, made it difficult to conceal at tea-time from those who wanted to come to a " party," but did not really care about music.

Eugene Goossens came to Edith Grove during this season and brought his two younger brothers, one of whom played the oboe with distinction, while the other played the French horn. Very valuable adjuncts they became to our musical life, those two lads, and it was sad to learn in after years that the youngest was killed in France during the earliest months of the war. They were both at that time members of Sir Arthur Wood's Symphony Orchestra and though only fifteen and seventeen years old, were considered accomplished musicians by their fellow members in the orchestra. Leon is still a member of that remarkable body of musicians. When we had a matter like the *Siegfried Idyll* in hand or a Beethoven septet, they rushed eagerly to our assistance. Eugene was legitimately proud of them. He was nineteen years old, or thereabouts, and his chief occupation was that of composing. Born in Belgium and brought up in a monastery, he came to England in his youth. He brought one of his earliest works, a skilful symphonic development of an old Chinese folk song, to Edith Grove for its first hearing. Scored for several instruments it was an exceptionally mature work for so young a composer and was listened to with high pleasure by as discriminating a musical audience as he could ask for. Bauer, Arbos, Rubinstein, Kochanski, Lionel Tertis, Thibaud, Cortot, and the white-gloved Chester. He later simplified this work, writing it for piano and violin or cello.

70

Landon Ronald, then conductor of the London Symphony Orchestra, Benno Moiseivitsch, with his graceful pianistic gifts, Rebecca Clark who was distinguishing herself by her able violin playing, Irene Scharrer playing the piano with sumptuous brilliance, Paul Kochanski reaching great heights of violin playing; Charles Draper with his flute (and oh! the solemnity with which one of the miracle maids used to announce that " Mr. Draper had telephoned to know if Mr. Draper had received Mr. Draper's music that Mr. Draper had sent to Mr. Draper's house for the evening's performance? "), Mr. Barrere with his flute, an Englishman who played the violin and his wife Edith who played the piano, (for the life of me I cannot remember more of their names, — from now on they must be Mr. and Mrs. Edith), Pedro Morales, a violinist of conflicting musical enthusiasm and melancholy depressions, Louis Persinger whose fine musicianship has since guided Yehudi Menuhin to the concert stage, — were some of the artists who, in addition to those already familiar, gave of their best with unstinted generosity and unflagging enthusiasm, to those evenings in Edith Grove. The year 1913–14 was to hold an even greater store of musical treasure, but this was becoming exciting enough.

Needless to say, they played through the night. It often occurred that an artist who did not live in London would arrive for the night of the concert only, leaving London the next day. This meant that he would not arrive at Edith Grove until after the concert and its tedious artist's-room salutations and compliments were terminated (though I never knew one who did not like them) anywhere between ten-thirty and midnight, and would not leave until it was time to catch the boat-train in the morning. He would find perhaps a movement from a Brahms violin sonata, a Beethoven trio for flute, violin, piano, a Chopin mazurka or German song cycle already in full swing and would creep into a chair or on a cushion until it was over. Then, usually hungry and a little tired from the strain of a concert, we would carry him off upstairs for food and drink. After which the really serious work of the evening would begin and continue until the skylight in the roof above us would turn from black to black-blue to blue-grey to yellow-grey and at last show clear blue sky beyond yellow sunlight, seen through blue-yellow-grey layers of smoke from burning wood, burning tobacco and burning candles. It would be six o'clock — seven o'clock — eight o'clock in the morning before we would make another visit to the dining-room, where the miracle maids after eight hours' sleep had somehow managed to clear away the débris of Chester's pink food and lonely parts of deserted fowl and make room for fresh coffee, scrambled eggs in an enormous chafing dish, raspberries and strawberries in big bowls. Oh! those English berries! We would breakfast, and break day by going to bed.

This morning departure of guests was a source of constant curiosity and astonishment to the neighbours in Edith Grove. Curtain after curtain would be raised, some surreptitiously and only a few inches, others with an angry snap their whole length, and sleep-distorted faces would lurk and look from the windows. Many and varied were the reports that went flying from house to house, culminating at laſt in the leaſt possible one of all, that those big cases did not carry musical inſtruments — not they! They carried all the wicked apparatus of gambling. No one could ſtay up all night to play music. Only for " vice " could they ſtay so long awake. Neighbours in the more immediate vicinity could, to their great misfortune, emphatically deny this. They *heard* music to the loss of their sleep and occasionally their tempers. Those at the back of our house, who slept with their windows open juſt over the also open skylight in the roof of 19A, were the moſt violent in proteſtation; even ſtaging a public demonſtration from window to window on one night, by blowing policemen's whiſtles, shooting off torpedoes, and filling the night air with hootings and rattles. They were answered by John Warner and Arthur Rubinſtein playing a Bach Prelude and Fugue for four hands on the piano. Bach is ſtirring enough played by two hands: by four, it is not conducive to sleep. May it here be recorded, however, that in the house adjoining number 19, there lived in an isolation which the exiſtence of two sad silent daughters under the same roof did not seem to invade, a crabbed old gentleman. And this old gentleman, upon his departure from London for the gentler life of the country, wrote us a letter of regret that he was giving up the only real pleasure he had extraſted from life in years, namely that of being a " privileged, though invisible liſtener to ſtrains of music of a kind hitherto undreamed of," and for which he

73

thereby desired to register his thanks. If only we had known.

Baroness von Hutten had a nose for parties and could smell Victor Watson's bass cello from the front door on the afternoon of one, even if it was concealed under the piano. Though she was as gracious a guest as she was a hostess, there were occasions upon which my heart sank when she entered the door, very particularly if they were musical. She knew very little about music and though sensitive to it in a generally appreciative way, she could utter the most arrogant nonsense in the way of learned opinion. Had she been content to take what pleasure from music her senses afforded her, she could have remained a decorative picture on the landscape or rather roomscape, but with determination she *would* discuss; and amiable as these artists were under my roof, they were occasionally forced into irritated retreat by her volubility. She was there, for instance, on the night already mentioned when Eugene's composition based on a Chinese folk song had its first performance. At its close, she stated calmly but with high-headed assertion amidst the general approbation, " All very nice, my dear boy, but the theme is not Chinese."

" I am sorry, dear madame," answered Eugene, with composure, " but it *is* Chinese."

" Dear boy, don't be foolish, because I *know* it's not."

" Baroness von Hutten, you are wrong," this with slightly less composure from Eugene. " It is one of the historical musical themes of China, taken from the one unquestionably authoritative work on the subject, which

74

has been the source of all we know of Chinese music for the laſt thousand years." His tone, for anyone else in the world, would have been final. Not so for the Baroness.

" Well, my child, you may think so, but I assure you it is not. You see, I have been there and I know."

What can be done in face of such an attitude? Plainly nothing but walk away, which is what Goossens did. A singing-teacher in this country, whose better known brother writes novels for those who can read them, talked to me like that for forty minutes one evening here in New York, not so very long ago, on the subjeſt of why Lenin had been " the bloodieſt tyrant and cut-throat ever known to hiſtory." Every time I queſtioned him as to the basic faſts upon which he formed his opinion, he would answer, " Well, you see, my brother was in the Secret Service during the war " (whose brother was not?) " and the Government gave him a yacht, and I've been out on that yacht, and I know." " Been *where* on it? " I asked. " Well, never mind, I've been *on* it. You see, my brother was in the Secret Service during the war and the Government gave him a yacht and I've been on it and I *know*." He had not been to Russia on that yacht — no. He juſt *knew* on that yacht. At the eleventh repetition of this, not being as wise as Eugene, I did not walk away. I shrieked, in violent hyſteria, " He *knows!* His brother was . . . " And then all I remember is that I found myself transported into a taxicab, with Guthrie McClintic saying very persuasively and gently, in a tone the perfeſt nurse adopts at the bedside of a delirious patient to whom she is about to adminiſter a sedative, " Here, Draper, read this — read it," and he pushed into my hand a newspaper clipping, which by the light of a fluttering match I read. It was Carl Sandburg's poem, *Flash Crimson*. I recovered. I have never dared to reread the poem. It may not be so good. Thank you, Guthrie.

To go back to Eugene Goossens. He talked even then of the orchestra he would one day conduct, and the programs he would build. He conducted Wagner's *Siegfried Idyll* for us, a work scored for seventeen instruments, from the perilous vantage of a soap box that threatened at every moment to overturn him, though it never threatened his calm. His fluency, sensitiveness and rhythmic subtlety were marked. His power and control increased from season to season. He has since fulfilled the promise of that early period and has builded better programs than any conductor of his years. From Bach to Brahms to Stravinsky to Mozart, or Beethoven to Mussorgsky to Strauss to Debussy, are familiar progressions of his. His devotion to the music of contemporary composers, his understanding of their work and the ability to convey his understanding to the men playing under him have proved significant aids to the clarification of otherwise confused performances. To his everlasting credit be it said that he risked everything he had in the way of money in founding an orchestra for the playing of modern works, and was alone responsible for the first performance of *Le Sacre du Printemps* as a symphonic work in England. In this manner has this curly-headed, gallant young Belgian won his way to the position he now holds as conductor of Mr. Eastman's orchestra at Rochester, an orchestra that bids fair to become one of the first in the country, unless some ambitious competitor snatches him away.

May Mukle, looking like a sturdy young gipsy, and playing with a controlled fervour unusual to her sex when faced with the tempting emotional possibilities of the cello, was often one of the collaborators in the Brahms sextets which became an accepted part of the winter's musical program, or the Schubert quintet for piano, violin, viola and cellos, which was played as often as time and circumstance allowed. It is to me one of the great musical compositions written for strings. At every fresh hearing, the immortal theme of the second movement and the noble poignancies of the closing movement as it reaches its climax, assume an increased importance for my ear and what lies beyond. Its greatest performance at Edith Grove was given by Thibaud, Lionel Tertis, Casals, Felix Salmond and Arthur Rubinstein. To one who knows the work, what more need be said? To one who does not, may life vouchsafe him the experience ere heaven offers him some lesser joy.

Lionel Tertis was unique among viola players. He made of that ungrateful but necessary instrument a solo instrument of manifold beauties and possibilities. Its heavily grained tone texture, which in less gifted hands presents an obstacle to be overcome or a limitation to be regretted, became for him the chief asset of his art. Every note was a full convinced statement that between the brilliant clarities and penetrating flexibilities of the violin and the rich serenities and shapely flow of the cello, was a province of sound where the qualities of both were accessible to one instrument, and that was the viola. Phrases given to the viola emerged with startling value when played by Tertis, instead of sinking anonymously into the general musical whole. Too fine an artist ever to intrude his virtuosity in ensemble playing, or over-emphasize by the tiniest fraction of a phrase the emotional power he could extract from it, he made a definite contribution to the structure of a work by the just importance he was able to give the viola part. Sonatas and one concerto for viola have been written for him to play, and more of his kind might encourage a real literature for the viola which at present it so conspicuously lacks.

So through the season of 1912–13 it went. No visiting musician left London without being brought to Edith Grove, and it went without saying that those who came to give concerts would come on to us afterward.

It was in 1913 that Paul Draper gave his first concert since studying with Mühlen. Mühlen announced that he was " having kittens of nervousness," and could not move from home. Before a distinguished audience Draper recorded his potentialities as the unequalled interpreter of German songs that he afterward became. A voice that had little natural " beauty " of tone became a perfected musical instrument through the sheer intelligence and austerity that Mühlen found there to work with. His use of voice as a symbol for what the composer endeavours to communicate was of the highest art, transcending by its very purity of purpose any lack of mere ear-titillation it might display. He had no more fervent admirers than Casals, Bauer, Thibaud, Rubinstein and Kochanski and later on in this country, Bodansky, Mahler, Muck and Stokowski. No mean audience to gain in one lifetime.

. . . .

During this season also there were bad moments. One was caused by the " pianist from Munich." No one is quite clear how he got there, and Draper would never confess what I am convinced was his share of responsibility in it. I only know that on an evening when many of us were gathered happily in the excavated house at 19A, trying out a new quartet of Emerson Whithorne's, when down the stairs came the most timid, apprehensive big figure of a man I have ever seen. Had he been small, he would not have looked so pathetic, but to witness fear and nervousness spread over so large an area was doubly distressing. He was preceded by one of the miracle maids who, diminutive as she was in stature, seemed a bulwark of courage and strength before him. She came straight to me, her poor victim hypnotized into following her, and announced firmly, " The gentleman Mr. Draper expects — the pianist from Munich," and then withdrew. I greeted him with what soothing cordiality I could muster and searched the room for Draper. He was standing in frowning perplexity far away by the piano, and I summoned him with as fierce a glance as my eyes are capable of. He came over to where I stood, and I said, " Paul, here is the nice gentleman you expect, the pianist from Munich." Up to this moment no word had been uttered by the big, sad man. I left him to Paul for a min-

79

ute, who gave no sign of recognition, though every pro-
testation of pleasure at seeing his friend, his great friend,
the gentleman he expected, the pianist from Munich.
The air was permeated with uneasiness. The reading of
Whithorne's quartet was halted, and I rallied all the
people there into a group to meet the great sad man, who
never vouchsafed us his name. We offered cigars, food, a
drink, a chair, the fire, a nap, anything, in fact, that anyone could think of to make him speak. He became increasingly affrighted and silently bigger. At last it occurred to me that the only thing we knew about him
might be the key that could unlock his terror. I would
ask him to play. I did.

His face lightened for a moment with an expression
which I uneasily interpreted as surprised gratitude. Everyone rushed to prepare the piano, glad to be freed from the
hypnotizing spell of his silent immovability. I muttered a
few imprecations to Draper under my breath in the op-
portunity thus afforded, and said, " In God's name, who
is he? Why didn't you warn me or have you never seen
him before? " " Don't be silly," he answered, " of course
I have seen him before. I know him quite well in fact, he
is very well known, but . . . I have forgotten his name.
He is a superb pianist." Somehow I knew he was lying.
He was determined to find a way out of the confusion for
himself. He certainly had never heard that man play the
piano, wherever or however he had met him; he had confused him with some never-to-be-ascertained really well-
known pianist from Munich. This, however, was no moment to discuss it, as the big sad man had seated himself

at the piano and was about to begin. The room quieted down, feeling this was either a great discovery or a great mystery. The pianist from Munich began. He played Schubert's *Marche Militaire*. With tears of emotion running down his cheeks and dripping off the end of his walrus moustache he played it, every repeat, every note. The *Marche Militaire!* At thirteen, being the promising pupil of the local piano teacher of the town where I was born, I played it at my first and last piano recital. It was the *pièce de résistance* of the program, which included besides, if I remember correctly, Mendelssohn's *Spring Song,* his *Spinning Song,* Nevin's *Venetian Suite,* and Sinding's *Rustle of Spring.* My sister-in-law gave me a bunch of pink roses, the only ones I ever received on a concert-stage, and my father gave me a look over his loudly clapping hands that made me realize that piano-playing was perhaps not, after all, to be my chosen *métier.* A good musician, my father. I had not heard the *Marche Militaire* very often since then. But there it was in my ears once again, played by the gentleman Mr. Draper expected, the pianist from Munich, in 19A Edith Grove. He played it through and stopped. We thanked him, we applauded, we thanked him again, and started upstairs to the dining-room, feeling that supper and supper alone could end the nightmare. He came with us, a little less sad, just as silent and, after refusing all food and drink, took his lonely departure. We fell upon Draper for an explanation. He had none. There never will be one.

Another evening Thibaud had telephoned me to ask if

he might bring a charming friend of his, a certain *Mme. Tel et Tel* who was an accomplished musician, and who so much desired to play in Edith Grove. I of course assented. I have never yet understood French over the telephone and though Thibaud assured me afterward that he explained carefully to me just what instrument she played, the subsequent events were nevertheless a complete surprise.

Thibaud came dashing down the stairs into 19A that night about eleven o'clock in a febrile excitement of spirits. Arthur Rubinstein was playing some new songs of Sczymanowski's, the *Hafiz Cycle,* and Paul Draper was reading them with the fervent pleasure every note written by that man always evoked. He was preparing to sing them during the next season and Rubinstein had offered to accompany him. Well — Thibaud dashed downstairs and in and up to me, saying: *"Bon soir, ma chère Muriel. Je vous présente ma très chère amie et grande musicienne Mlle."* — here he paused, looked over his shoulder and seeing no one following him continued — " *ma très chère amie et grande musicienne, Mlle. . . ."* Again he turned to look at the staircase. There, halfway down appeared a harp, a beautiful golden harp. It did not move. Behind its strings, as if from a prison in heaven, an enormous black mass was discernible, and just over one corner of it a frightened white fat face of general feminine contour emerged.

" *Monsieur Thibaud,"* it cried. " *Venez à mes secours. Je ne peux pas bouger. Venez m'aider, je vous en prie."*

Thibaud leapt up the stairs to her *secours,* and began

82

making every attempt to move the harp and the lady, to no avail. We all rushed to the staircase and the aid of the imprisoned young female. It could not be done. The harp had lodged itself in some inextricable way diagonally across the staircase. The lady's bulk prevented its being moved backwards, and her devotion to her instrument prevented our moving it forward. What to be done? The lady began to cry. Truly she was in an unbecoming predicament. It was decided that if only Thibaud could get on the other side of the harp with her he might pacify her and so direct her movements as to allow a descent or at least a retreat. We opened a rarely used door concealed behind the huge folds of the Kien Lung screen and let him out, *pushed* him out is really the word, and he flew to the front door of 19, was let in, and appeared almost immediately at the lady's side; not exactly side, but somewhere behind her. After a number of strategic moves of harp and lady, accompanied by a comforting chatter that was punctuated by unholy wit, he managed to extricate her, save the harp, and bring them both somehow into the room. Then he turned to me once more and as if nothing had happened began all over again from the beginning, saying, " *Bon soir, ma chère Muriel. Je vous présente ma très chère amie et grande musicienne, Mlle. X,"* whatever her name was. It was perfect. Unfortunately, the lady was too upset to make any demonstration of musicianship, and anyway he never told me she played a harp. No telephone, even on the continent, could have concealed that calamity from me.

I would like to arrange a concert to be given by her

and the pianist from Munich. I would add one more artist
to that program. She sang. It happened this way. A peren-
nially young, fair-haired little English woman, who believed everybody and everything and got younger every
year on it, asked if she could bring a " thrilling Russian-
Irish mystic, a fascinating lady who sings " to the house
one evening. Eagerly anticipating such a combination,
I arranged for her to come to the next party, which would,
I hoped, be one of welcome to Karol Sczymanowski, on
his way to London at last. Karol did not arrive that night,
but she did. A stark, gaunt, thin, big-boned female, more
Irish than Russian and more heavily veiled than mystic,
strode into the room in the wake of the blonde, tripping
little English lady. She was presented to me, and with an
accent whose genealogy I would hesitate to trace, she began to say the usual things. How good of me, how beautiful an atmosphere I created, how she longed to sing to
me, etc., etc., etc. A little suspicious, I asked a kindly soul
if she would accompany her (it was Mrs. Edith), and a
song was chosen by the Russian-Irish mystic. It was *Ich
Grolle Nicht* by Schubert, and with Draper frowning disapproval, the performance began. After much fussing
and fuming, she placed herself between the piano and the
music shelves which were built against the wall just beyond it. On top of these shelves, high enough to be out of
the way of anyone but a Russian-Irish mystic, was a much
prized collection of Canton enamel vases, candle-sticks,
boxes and incense burners. Well, she began to sing, that
woman, with a fury and intensity that I have never heard
or seen equalled. The whole structure of the song and its

84

meaning was entirely lost, in fact, completely contra-
dicted, by this woman's " mystic " fervour. She waved her
very long strong arms in every possible direction, almost
shaking her fist as she declared paradoxically enough,
Ich Grolle Nicht. Mrs. Edith was in danger: she could
evade it; but it was soon evident that so was the Canton
enamel, which could not. At the final climax of the song,
which was transformed into an angry denial of everything, with one far-flung gesture of the arms, the singer
struck out for the pieces of Canton enamel. She made
them, and with an all-embracing gesture swept them to
the floor, where they fell with a sickening crash not loud
enough, however, to drown out that last *Ich Grolle
Nicht.* She waited for applause and got it. I clapped
loudly. I have never seen such a performance, to say
nothing of hearing one, in my life. The young-old little
English lady murmured apologetically, " My dear, I'm
so sorry, but she *is* mystic really." The accompanist rose
up from the débris of shattered vases. Draper, avenged
for his pianist from Munich, put several logs on the fire,
and again we went up to supper — blessed interlude.
Yes, she would make a fine third for that concert.

.   .   .   .

Karol Sczymanowski did arrive a fortnight later; his
close friends, Paul and Sozia Kochanski and Arthur
Rubinstein, practically bringing him in their arms. Aloof,
sensitive, secure, shy, he walked into the room and lifted a
beautiful head from retreating hovering shoulders. Features of nobility were brushed with gentle strokes of
silvery-gold sadness. Generations of Polish submission

looked out from fathomless eyes, and generations of
Polish rebellion moulded his forehead. Mobile lips shaped
words into subtly chiselled silver images as he spoke. He
brought with him the world of ecstatic suspense in which
he lives and creates, protecting it with those embracing
hovering shoulders and obliquely lowered head. From the
moment he arrived at Edith Grove he became one of the
most dearly loved people in it. He had projects, or rather
his friends had for him (for he occupied himself little
with such events), concerning the production of his
opera, which had had its première in Cracow the previous
season. Rubinstein played the score through for us that
night. It is an important and lovely work. Why is it, and
its successor, neglected here in the vast dearth of contemporary operas that exists? However, there he was. His
song cycles sung by Draper in concert had made him
known amongst a few, and of course musicians knew already of his First Symphony. They made much of him,
though he made nothing of himself. He simply was.

. . . .

At Mrs. Napier's house one day I met Henry James.
I must either pause here for two years and write a book, or
just jump bravely in. So, I repeat, at Mrs. Napier's house
one day in 1913 I met Henry James. Since a day when, as
a small child, I sat unnoticed in a room in which a great
woman, Elizabeth Cummings, was reading aloud to my
mother, I had wanted to meet Henry James. The book
was *What Maisie Knew* (didn't I say I was unnoticed?)
and after a particularly dazzling passage Elizabeth Cummings had paused. My mother looked up from her sew-

ing and exclaimed, "How does he manage to bring about such a thing!" and Elizabeth Cummings answered, "He doesn't manage, my dear Susan; he is a genius." The functionings of genius presented a problem beyond my power to solve, but the effect the word had on me was magical. I rose from the corner where I had been sitting in guilty quiet, and asked, "Is he alive?" Disturbed by my presence, Elizabeth Cummings put the book down; alarmed by my voice, my mother said "Yes." After a nervous pause I was sent from the room on some needless errand, bearing within me a firm resolve, which was that if there was one genius still alive (at that age, one always thinks of them as dead — indeed it is a delusion from which many people never recover), I must somehow manage to see him.

Many years passed and I saw him. Though by that time perfectly aware that still other geniuses were alive, I could never quite dissociate him in my mind from the reverent amazement I had felt upon first hearing that a genius lived in the same world with myself. He stood, a solid squared ashlar of wisdom, with a magnificently domed head atop, in Mrs. Napier's drawing-room. I walked up to him as bravely as I could, and we met. I told him how it had come about that he had entered my childhood as a uniquely living genius. He listened, with a burdened smile on his full lips, he who had to hear so much, and then it began. With a labouring that began stirring in the soles of his feet and worked up with Gargantuan travail through his knees and weighty abdomen to his heaving breast and strangled column of a throat, hoisted up by eyebrows raised high over the most steadily watching eyes I have ever looked into, he spoke. Having imaginatively participated in every effort his body had made, I was exhausted by the time the words were finally born, but had awaited them too long not to rally my attention when I heard them. They were about like this:

" My dear, — if I may call you so, my dear, — my even now — if I may yet further without permission so invade your, to be sure, passing years — child, my dear child. How right and yet how perfectly — if perfection can so enter, how perfectly wrong they both were, *you* were, all of you were."

I sat down. He sat beside me, and in a kind of mutual agony, we continued. I was later to discover that there was a way of communication with him that avoided all this amazing difficulty, which allowed the rich vein of his knowledge of human beings and events to flow unchecked, and which made listening to him and talking with him one of the rare values of my life, but this first time was agony. Again and again, in that memorable conversation, he would raise those cornices of eyebrows in an effort to build under them the astounding structure of words that so decorate his written page, and again and again would fail to find them. He seemed to listen for them with his own ear as eagerly as I with mine and even kept his eye alert for the possible shape of one that might appear by happy accident. Rejecting any less felicitous expression of his thought than one that would perfectly convey it, he would throw one phrase after the other away on its tremendous journey up from the soles of his feet.

A patient " er — er — er " was the only sign that another had fallen by the wayside. Once, with temerity, I offered him one, almost beseeching him to take it as agreed counterfeit until such time as real gold would be passed over the counter and this soul-racking barter cease. But no, with the dear heavy smile leaving his lips to rest for a moment somewhere under his eyes, he cast it aside. So it went. The weight of his thought, the penetrating justice of his wit, and the impact of his whole being were such that I would gladly have suffered the pain of its articulation through years of silence, had they not seemed to me also " to be sure, passing years."

We spoke of America a little tentatively, a little anxiously and very tenderly. We spoke of families. He heard there was a son. He wanted to know him. He spoke of Ruth Draper and her talent. He spoke of music and asked to come one night to Edith Grove and listen. And then, as I pulled myself up and away from his side, fascinated, exhausted and adoring, his eyes travelled up from under the corniced eyebrows and saw my hat. It was a small white satin affair, with a cluster of tiny white love birds perched at the front. He gasped with horror, pointed his finger, and said with utter kindness, " My child," (it came easier this time), " my very dear child — the cruelty — ah! the cruelty of your hat! That once living — indeed yes, loving, — creatures should have been so cruelly separated by death to become so unhappily and yet, ah! how becomingly united on your hat."

I had met Henry James!

Soon after he came to lunch. Crossing the threshold of Edith Grove, he questioned me as to the tenure of the house. How long a lease did we have? How long would we be there? I told him it was a twenty-one-year lease and he sighed ponderously, saying, " Long enough to see me out, my child, long enough to see me out. Stay me out, I beg — stay me out." He had asked to be quite alone, so Paul and I sat one on either side of him and listened. After lunch he and I went down to the studio through the staircase where the lady harpist had remained so long imprisoned. He asked to see my son, so that young person was sent for. The Irish angel brought him. He was only a little over three years old, and a few days before had been found asleep with a copy of Henry James' book, *Letters of a Son and Brother,* under his pillow, his hand slipped in at a page upon which a photograph of Henry and his brother William standing close to their father's knee was reproduced. The tale of this incident had moved Henry James and when my son came into the room he fastened his accurately wise eye upon him. The Irish angel had brushed his hair until it shone, and dressed him in his best afternoon raiment, which consisted of long linen trousers and suspenders cut out of one piece, fastened to a frilled white shirt at the shoulders by a huge pearl button. The devouring James focused his gaze on that button and held it there as the child crossed the vast room. Spontaneously glad to see this grown-up who in his youth had leaned so trustingly at his father's knee, my son had entered the room on the run, but faced with the arresting force of his gaze, his footsteps faltered and his pace slackened, so that by the time he came to within three feet of Henry James, he stopped short and remained motionless as that great man began to address him:

"Ah! my boy. So here you come, faithfully — as it were, into view — with buttons, yes, *buttons* . . ." Here he paused while the yeast that would eventually give rise to the ultimate word began to ferment in the soles of his feet: as it reached his knees he repeated, "Buttons, that are, er — that are — er er . . ." By this time the poor child was intimidated by the intensity of tone and started to back away, but Henry James began a circular movement in air with the forefinger of his right hand and continued — "buttons that have been — er," — and then in a shout of triumph — "*jettés-D,* as it were, yes, *jettés-d,*" — his voice quieting down as the word emerged, — "*jettés-d* so rightly, so needfully, just there, my child," pointing in the direction of his small shoulder. But my child heard him not. At the first burst of "*jettés-D*" he had fled terrified from the room, the discovery of which brought forth from Henry James the mournful reflection, "Would I had remained a photograph!"

To be called to the telephone by Henry James was an experience in itself. The first time it happened I, all unaware, took up the receiver eagerly, and said, "Yes — this is Muriel."

A voice that began to twist and turn on the other end of the wire, finally spoke.

"Would you be — er — or rather, my dear, — er —

my very dear, if I may call you so, child, would you, — not by — er — er *arrangement,* but would you — more — er — truthfully speaking — be — er — er NATU- RALLY at home — this afternoon?."

By that time I was not naturally anything at all, and could only gasp, "Yes, always, any time — yes, yes, this afternoon at five, I will, unnaturally or not, be here — yes," and hung up.

It was during this visit that I learned to talk with him and listen to him, by withdrawing the weight of my at- tention from his actual words and the anguished facial contortions that accompanied them, and fastening it on the stream of thought itself. I even diverted my eyes from that part of his face from which the phrases finally emerged, namely, his mouth, and directed them to a more peaceful spot between his eyes, which I imagined to be the source of thought. It proved helpful. Evidently released from some bondage which the eye and ear of a listener imposed upon him, he seemed to feel more free. My effort to ignore the words and extract the meaning by a sense of weight, inflection and rhythm which em- anated from him, removed the burden he must have felt at keeping me — anyone — waiting so long, and gradually the full current of his thought was flowing steadily, pauses and hesitations becoming accents rather than impediments. It proved an excellent *modus operandi* from then on, and only at those times when he had an audience of more than one person did the old difficulties return.

A few nights after this lunch, Thibaud, Casals, Rubinstein, Kochanski and Sczymanowski were to be the nucleus of an evening at Edith Grove; so I sent a line to Henry James informing him of this and begging him to join us. He arrived early and sledged down the stairs into the room with that extraordinary density of movement that was characteristic of him. He did not give the impression of putting one foot before the other in order to carry his torso and its appendages into the room. He came in all at once. Head, shoulders, arms, body, legs, arrived at the same time, inexorably displacing space and leaving an almost visible vacancy in his wake. Solid purposeful wholeness impelled him. All of him was there, nothing left behind. He sat quietly on the sofa beside me and awaited silently the first notes of the Brahms B Major piano trio which was to begin the evening's program. As the music progressed and the incomparable tone of Casals' cello was heard in the short solo passage of the first movement, his solemnly searching eyes fastened on Casals' face, and he seemed to listen by seeing. When Thibaud began the brilliant passage for violin in the second movement, his eyes left Casals, as if he had drunk him all in through his organs of sight — music, hands, bowing and all — and centred on Thibaud, whom he watched with meticulous care during the whole second movement. During the last, when Arthur Rubinstein was burning the music out of the piano with an accumulating speed that left even those great artists somewhat breathless as he rushed them up to the high climax of the trio, H. J. turned the attention of his listening eyes toward him and kept it there until the performance came to a close. Only then did he begin to question me and greet one or two of the artists as they came up. His need for exhaustive analysis of each one separately made it difficult for him to take them in collectively, and I left him talking tortuous French to Thibaud. Casals was clamouring for the Schubert octet which was his favourite, as the Mendelssohn was Thibaud's. He said " one drank fresh milk " in listening to it, and could he please hear it through instead of playing it. As soon as enough artists had arrived to make up the necessary parts, it began — Thibaud, playing first violin, Bauer and Mr. Edith playing second violins, (yes, Bauer, whose great pleasure it occasionally was when circumstance allowed, to play the violin in a familiar work), one of the Goossens boys playing the horn, Harold Bauer's sister Gertrude playing viola, Rubio playing the cello, the faithful Watson double-bass, a friend of his snatched from back-stage by the method outlined earlier in this narrative, playing the clarinet. Casals sat on one side of me smoking a huge cigar, which was one of his few indulgences, and Henry James on the other, watching, absorbing, recording every gesture and expression of each man or woman in the room, and each object or article of furniture in relation to them. His appreciation was for and in terms of images. No sounds passed unsifted through that battery of image attention he so skilfully employed.

He seemed to be possessed of an inner secret delight. It was as if he were playing a powerful game of the intellect, a game the rules of which he had himself invented, the honours of which were unalienably his. It appeared to absorb, amuse, and frighten him a little as well. Fright could have been lessened only at the cost of diminished absorption and amusement, a price he would not pay.

He took in the fragile, minute and blonde delicacy of Mme. Thibaud as she sat in timorous sprightliness in an enveloping armchair of exaggerated dimensions, under a vase of heavily blossoming, formally petalled pink and white camellias, gleamily bending through glossy dark green leaves. He did not neglect Mme. Suggia, the gifted cello-playing friend of Casals before he married Susan Metcalf, who sat in swarthy gold, white, and black of dress and skin and hair on a small upright Chinese Chippendale chair in the spectral shadow of paling almond flowers. He saw the sensitive aloof protection which Karol Sczymanowski threw about himself and the life-defying speed with which Arthur Rubinstein managed to stand still. To all this he gave the steady orderliness of his observation. Toward the end of the octet, Montague Vert Chester, in a new pair of white gloves, came into the room. As was the unvarying custom at Edith Grove he crept into the nearest seat he could find without even a whisper of greeting, and listened with the rest. It happened to be a seat on the other side of James, and when the music was over, I presented him. " Chester, this is Mr. James." Chester, with a scant nod, for he had no social grace, said, " Good evening, Mr. James," and began to talk across him to me. Knowing that Chester admired his works with an enthusiasm that he rarely accorded anything other than music, my son and pink food, I

95

added, "Mr. Henry James, Chester." He bounded up from his seat and shouted with excitement:

"What, not *the* Mr. James? Not the great Henry James?" offering his white-gloved hand in clumsy respect, eyes popping from his head.

From under benevolent eyebrows *the* Mr. James looked up and said soothingly, "Take it gently, my good man, take it gently."

Chester sat down.

In a corner formed by three folds of the Kien Lung screen, lighted by a Burmese chandelier of carved golden flowers and leaves that trailed downward over her head, I had placed a Chinese stone statue of the Goddess of Charity. Her right arm held in calm closeness to her side under gracious folds of modest raiment, her left hand outstretched to offer a basket filled with fruits of human kindness, eyes drooping to veil from sight the need of those who took, she stood forever in impassioned serenity. It was to Henry James a source of unending wonder. Standing before it the first time, he turned to me and chanted:

"Ah! My child, what a lesson to the artists of to-day on where to begin and to the women of to-day on where to leave off!"

So I could go on for pages, but as it has been decided that this is not to be a book on Henry James, I offer this mere handful of impressions caught at random from the air he so invaded. I will add that when fate determined that I should leave London during 1915, I saw him one long last time. Invalided, sickened with a grief and distress that need no retelling, he heard my news. After an unforgettable silence, he said:

" So, my child, my very dear child, you are not staying me out. You are returning to that America we . . ." Here his pause was not for lack of words, but the more clearly to convey the unspoken. And then — " Ah! Well — perhaps one day I may do some faint far justice to all this," — with a wave of the arm that encircled the room and everything that had ever been seen, spoken or heard in it — " to all this you have given me — to all this," and he patted my hand. He did not say good-bye, but sledged slowly sadly wisely out, the domed head disappearing like a silvered sun at the top of the stairs. I never saw him again.

.   .   .   .

John Sargent I met that winter at the studio of H. Harris Brown. He was making charcoal drawings of Ruth Draper, who was staying with us, and I went to his studio one morning to watch their progress. A shy, big, gentle, blood-filled face, black eyes, constantly moving hands that drew volutes in the air, an advancing-retreating walk, he ushered me into the room. The sketch of Ruth Draper already begun was far from successful. Not having " seen " her monologues, he was making a plain statement of her face with no indication of its remarkable ability to reproduce each and every emotion a human being can experience. He became restless as he worked, and must have felt a disturbance of wings in the air from some uncaptured thing in flight. After two or three more sittings, he sent the finished portrait to her, and though it had the nice virtuosity of draughtsmanship his quick sketches often displayed, it was not essentially a portrait. Some time after this he came to Edith Grove on a night when she was reciting and ſtood leaning againſt the panel of the door at the bottom of the ſtairs, watching her intently, indeed furiously, with blood-suffused face and eyes. The next morning she received word from him to deſtroy the portrait, throw it in the Thames, do anything she liked with it, but not accept it as his portrait of her. Now that he had " seen " her, would she sit once more? This she did, and the two really fine drawings of her, one as the Scotch immigrant and the other as the Roumanian peasant, were the result.

He was a delightful host, and a party at his house was an event. On one wall of his big room hung the " Portrait of Mlle. X," now placed at the end of one of the galleries of the Metropolitan Museum. Dear Henry James, sitting beside me one night at Sargent's house, began telling me the ſtory of the infuriated mother of " Mlle. X," who had returned the portrait, not exaĉtly poſt-haſte, but as faſt as so large a canvas could be returned, with a note in which she expressed her outrage that so great an artiſt should have made a " portrait lubrique de ma fille." Dear James was explaining that " the dress, you see, cut a little perhaps generously, and held by such slender promises of modeſty across her shoulders " (she should have had buttons, *jettés-d,* as it were, so rightly, on those shoulders!) — was upsetting to the good lady, her mother, when he observed that my own frock was held in place by nothing more than

Portrait of Henry James by John Sargent

two strands of blue pearls, one on each shoulder. In extreme agitation lest I should pursue the analogy, he launched into the most elaborate discussion and comparison of clothes then and " now," plunging further and further in his desire to free my mind of any disapproving conclusion. His antics were endearingly elaborate, but his entanglement became so complex that I finally extricated him by saying, " I think it must have been the face she objected to." His courtesy, kindness and humour were high lights that played on the surface of his profound wisdom, intellectual clarity and micrometric interest in the conflicts and consummations that men and women bring about by living in the same world.

Sargent had a friend and ardent admirer in H. Harris Brown, called " Colour-Sergeant Brown " by some less kindly disposed acquaintances. Sargent was often to be found in his studio, and endless discussions ensued concerning paints — mixing them, laying them on, varnishing them, cleaning them, and taking them off. This would go on by the hour, to their mutual delight. " Brownie " is the one portrait-painter I ever heard Sargent recommend, if I may call it so. When he had more commissions than he could execute (and when had he not?), he would say, " Why don't you go to Brown? He will paint you a damned fine portrait." Many did and it was possibly the turning-point in the career of this hard-working, serious, admirable artist, whose portraits of popes, prime ministers, princesses and plain people, to say nothing of Red Indians, are familiar to his New York public.

He was and is a person of indomitable energy, inextinguishable childlike gaiety and sudden bursts of temper. Motoring to the country for a week-end at "The House in the Woods," Baroness von Hutten's charming country-place, a large party of us, including Brownie, met with mishap after mishap. This led to strained nerves, snapping irritation or sulky silence on the part of most of us. Tires burst, routes were missed, engines went wrong, rain poured in torrents and finally the car in which Brownie and myself, Emerson Whithorne and the Baroness were sitting, went off the road and straight into a towering sandpile which was being used in some construction work by the roadside. There the car stuck and as far as anyone could see or any effort the chauffeur could make, there it would remain, perhaps forever. This was the last blow. I swore like a trooper, the Baroness wept, and Whithorne sulked. Only Brownie was imperturbable. Gazing rapturously through driving sheets of rain at the mountain of sand directly in front of us, he exclaimed joyously, "Oh! I say. What jolly sand!"

He painted a portrait of me, beginning it the first year we were in London and then laying it aside in despair (I am not a good " sitter ") until such time as I could find the patience to stand still long enough to complete it. This was not until the last week of my London life. He had worked on it by himself from time to time in the interim and only needed one or two more sittings to finish it. As an inducement, he brought Sargent to his beautiful studio in Mulberry Walk, Chelsea, for the laſt sitting and somehow it was finished, Sargent and Brownie walking me up and down in the dear English garden which Brownie had lovingly planted around his house, to refresh my flagging spirits. A ſtrange sight it muſt have been at eleven o'clock in the morning: Brownie in a paint-ſtained linen duſter, Sargent in brown and reds, like his face, and I wrapped in the unfortunate blue-silver cloth held up by those two ſtrands of blue pearls that had so diſtressed Henry James, with a burſt-ing blue osprey springing up out of my forehead. Do not ask where that portrait is. I said he was a man of sudden temper.

It was in that same ſtudio of noble fat Georgian proportions (H. H. Brown was possessed of a superior architeċtural sense, and had designed and supervised every cornice, ceiling, doorway and fireplace that had gone into his house, to say nothing of the house itself) that I met George Moore. A gentle clumsy waving filled the air as he approached. It seemed to pervade his whole person but upon close observation could be discerned as confined to his hands. Pulled forward by this hand-waving was a ponderous and somehow porous pink-and-white old baby face. The rest, I suppose, followed, though I can only see his face and hands. Eyes filled with blue-green-grey watery greed and sly attention floated through the general waving and scrutinized whatever objeċt was put before it. This time it happened to be me, and as Brownie presented him, this scrutiny provoked a whispered comment in the form of a query addressed to his hoſt concerning me . . . but alas! as audible as all ill-

meant whispers are. I saved Brownie the witless embar-
rassment of an answer by patting George Moore on the
shoulder and saying, " There, there, don't let it bother
you. Those who no longer can, must always hope the
worst for those who do." His eyes became angrily dry for
a second, and then he said abruptly:

" So you like Brahms? " But he never forgave me.
Years afterward — but that is another story. It does not
belong to the London that ended in 1914.

We discussed Brahms a little and Christ much. He was
in the preliminary throes of *Brook Kerith*. When I say
we discussed, I mean I listened. But the drying and wa-
tering of the eyes interested me much more than what
he said, which was trivial of me, but I suppose I was
angry too and could not listen. Very unsatisfactory meeting, except for the invigorating salt of his strong dislike,
always a flattery. The woman in him resented me. I decided just to keep on reading him and put myself down
as minus one valuable friendship in life, for surely he
is one of the few people left in the world who can still
write the English language.

. . . .

Which brings me to Norman Douglas. Norman Douglas has been part of my life since I met him at Capri on
my first trip abroad in the year 1906. He should be another book, another two years, but again I will jump in.
Brought to Europe under the vigilant chaperonage of
that same Elizabeth Cummings who read *What Maisie
Knew* to my mother, and a Mrs. Webb whose daughter
had married one of my brothers, I arrived at Capri with

them, and was installed in a villa which Mrs. Webb took for the winter months, called the *Torre Quattro Venti.* It belonged to old Elihu Vedder, the painter, and was just at the foot of the road that left Capri for Anacapri. In actual fact not only four, but the four and forty winds of heaven and hell howled round it day and night and must, I think, have affected the lives of those who lived in it. Mrs. Webb was actuated by the kindest impulses of wanting me to " see life," broaden my outlook, leave what to her were the desolate banks of the Merrimac River, Sinding's *Rustles of Spring* and the general provincial American scene, to live in the great civilization of Europe. Laudable desire. So I left the home of the most distinguished people I have ever known, my mother and my father, and the life that had poured through their ever-open doors since before I was born, and was taken to Capri.

I met Norman Douglas there and he gave me a glimpse of Joseph Conrad, but the rest of life at Capri would put the Merrimac River standards of provincialism to shame. (And, by the way, I met Paul Draper in Brookline.) However, what are a few deprivations and provincialisms in the scales against a Norman Douglas? I saw him for the first time one late afternoon at the foot of the villa stairs (there were a hundred forty-four to be climbed) as he was walking down the Anacapri road. I was between these two good ladies, Mrs. Webb and Elizabeth Cummings, and they seemed anxious to keep me there as this rugged sensitive figure greeted them in one of the most iridescent male voices I have ever heard. He

spoke rapidly but very distinctly, with a slight shaping
of his words on his underlip, that just escaped a lisp. The
infinitely varied inflections of his voice rose and fell on
a constantly sliding scale so that even his pauses were a
vibrating sound-bridge between words. It was magic,
and I was enchanted. He looked old enough to my
youthful mind to make it seem a little unkind of those
two dear ladies to keep me so buttressed. There was, for
instance, a young Count with whom they often left me
alone. . . . And here was this one, with a terrifyingly
intelligent humorous gleam in his eye, a nice Merrimac
Valley kind of walking stick in his hand such as my
father used to walk to early Communion with on Sunday morning, an indescribably rich " know " flowing
from him, and that voice! Something had to be done
about it. So I did something. I said, from between those
two virtuously flanking ladies, in a rather gasping voice,
" Won't you come to tea? "

He looked at me for a searching moment.

" Tea? No," he said; " but I will take you to see some
trees, the only real trees there are on this hellish little
island. Come along."

And regardless of the restraining arms and reproving
voices of those two good ladies, I just slipped out from
between them and . . . went, never daring to look
back.

" That's a good girl. You shouldn't sit up in that cold
hole drinking tea. *Tea,* my God! Who let you come over
here with those two old women? American parents don't
know the first thing about bringing up children. Have

you read *Plutarch's Lives?* Do you learn a column of the dictionary every day by heart? Well, you should. Tea, indeed — come along . . . I suppose you've met the Count? I might have known! My God! "

So we went, stumbling and scolding, along the road. When we reached the little grand opera piazza of Capri we struck off through some arcades and onto a stony path that went straggling up a hill. Everybody walks in Capri, and we passed several members of that motley crew of English, Danish, Polish, German, American estrays who people the island and chatter from tea-party to tea-party. Most of them I had met and, therefore, greeted them in passing. Each salutation brought forth some lively comment from Douglas, and ribald criticism of the social standards of Mrs. W. and E. C.

" So, you know that old thieving harlot, do you? I don't care if she *is* very well known in America. Look out for your purse and your lovers when she's about. Haven't got any? Well, you *should* have. Oh! These American parents! " And another passed. . . . " Beware of that young Danish doctor now. He is here because he just murdered his old uncle for a paltry thousand pounds. . . . Yes, he did too."

And still another.

" Frantic for three days she's been, that one, because she's expecting a new supply of drugs on the Naples boat and it hasn't come. The captain is probably holding it up for blackmail. Nice place you've picked in which to finish your education. Where *are* your parents, if you have any, which I'm beginning to doubt . . . Where

105

are they? I'll write them a letter and give them what-for.
No, I won't. Serve them right if you come back a mur-
derer, a drug fiend and a thief, to say nothing of . . .
Ah, well, never mind. Come along."

And I came along.

Finally, the stony little path stopped before a gate in a
high wooden fence. Douglas took a key out of his pocket,
put it in a lock of the gate in front of us, turned it, opened
the gate and pushed me in.

" There," he said. " There are some trees — the only
ones on the island. You call all these orange stands trees?
Go in there and look at these — I own them. They, and
the land they grow on, are the only things I own in
the world. I'll come back and get you when I think
you've been there long enough," and he shut the gate in
my face, turned the key in the lock and started down the
path muttering, " Tea, my God, tea! " as he walked
away.

I went into the trees.

That my first impressions of him are more easily conveyed in terms of his conversation than in physical description is possibly due to the tremendous word asso-
ciation that I have subsequently formed about him, as
his writings have developed into important contribu-
tions to English literature. At that time he was beginning
to write for publication, his life previous to this having
divided itself into separate eras of activity of about twelve
years' duration. His first twelve years were spent in
growing up. His second twelve years were dedicated to
music; he is an accomplished and true musician. His

next twelve were spent in diplomatic service which took him to many countries, and acquainted him with many languages. His years between thirty-six and forty-eight were largely years of specific study and investigation of facts geological, zoological and archeological: facts which formed a basis for certain erudite pamphlets he compiled in later years. These pamphlets are collector's items to-day and very scarce, as they were written by a scholar for scholars, and never intended for a public who likes to take its science in the form of society-column notes on the comings and goings of colonies of fish, the private life of whales, or the venereal diseases of minerals. From these pamphlets he wandered into the paths of short-story writing, and so on to the works which have made him famous amongst English speaking and reading peoples, books like *Old Calabria, Siren Land* and *South Wind.* The creating of these books occupied a good twelve years, from forty-eight to sixty, and will I trust continue to occupy his remaining ones. May he come to America before they close. His varied accumulation of knowledge of the past and present, of land and sea, of flesh and blood, untainted by anthropomorphism, his satirical impatience with shams and shibboleths, and his steadily maintained scale of values would be salutary weapons to use against us in this, our critical, period. His style and simplicity of language in using these weapons through the medium of the written word would be a grateful addition to the literature of our times. What a columnist he would make after a month or two spent in New York!

At the time I met him, twenty years ago, he was in the full flower of his geological investigations, and thus built a fence around the few remaining trees of Capri to watch them die. He was making his earliest essay into the field of short stories, and had published a volume of them, if I remember correctly. The first printed words of Norman Douglas's I ever saw were " But Alberique had fainted away." It was the last sentence of a story cut from a bound book and shown me in loose-leaf form. I remember thinking it very wicked and sophisticated at the time, though I have only the vaguest recollection of its plot — something to do with a young man playing a violin to a fascinating lady or a young lady playing a violin to a fascinating man. From his shyness in showing it to me (and Douglas is not a shy man, as you may have gathered), in spite of the fact that I had read neither *Plutarch's Lives* nor learned a column of the dictionary by heart every day, and from the fact that it was singled out from others, I imagine that he cherished it for some personal reason, but that his fine critical judgment had rejected them all.

This is getting worse than Henry James. I could stay for years locked up in his fenced-in property and ponder about his writing, but he did come back to get me. With a loud rapping of his cane on the high gate, he called out:

" American girl, who hasn't read *Plutarch's Lives* and has asked me to tea, are you there? . . . Well, come along then," and he turned the key in the lock and let me out. Together we walked back to the *Torre*

Quattro Venti. At the foot of the hundred forty-four steps I suggested that it were as well if he did not accompany me to the door. " No fear," he answered. " I wouldn't face those two witches to-night for anything you could offer me! Mind you learn a column of the dictionary to-night by heart, and to-morrow I'll come take you for another walk," and he waved his cane in the air and walked quickly away.

We will draw a curtain over my reception by the two good ladies. Dear unique Elizabeth Cummings, who had told my mother that Henry James did not manage because he was a genius, was, I could see, secretly delighted that I had taken matters into my own hands, and only fictitiously stern because she felt it her duty to be, as my moral guardian. Too brilliant and discerning a woman not to realize from my defensive description and her own observation of him, that he was a most unusual and rare person, she became mollified and curious at once, and said, " We'll ask him to tea to-morrow." " Couldn't we make it dinner or lunch? " I begged; " somehow, I don't think he likes tea." So it was arranged, and the next day a note was dispatched, but before it could have been received, one arrived from him to me.

" Dear Mew (that is all I understood of your name), I can't come take you for a walk to-day. I must go see Conrad who is here and ill. He has learned his dictionary and has excellent whisky. I enclose the key to the trees, if you want to go by yourself. Yours, and Aunt Eliza's (which is all I understand of your duenna's name), in Jesus, N. D."

Through the months I spent in Capri he was my guide, philosopher and friend. So he has remained through all the ensuing years, regardless of those that have passed without word or sight of me. Five of them had elapsed before I saw him again in London. He was at that time assistant editor of the *English Review,* a periodical that had passed through diverting and illustrious vicissitudes to come at last into the editorial hands of Austin Harrison. When I learned of Douglas' presence in London I sped him a note as follows:

" Dearest Doug: I have married, marrow, Mars, marsala, Marseillaise, marsh, marshal, marchalsea, marsupial, mart, martello, marital, Martin Paul Draper and live at 19 Edith Grove, grovel, grow, growl, growth, groyne, grub, grudge, gruel, gruesome, gruff, grumble, grume, grummet, grumpy, Grundyism, grunt, gruyere, grysbok. Will you come to tea, teach, teague, teak, teal, teamster, teapoy, tear, tearing, tease, teasel, technic at once (I have got some excellent whisky), and stay to dine, ding, dong, dinghey, dingle, dingo, dinosaur, dinothere, dint, diocese, dioptric, dioxide, dip — Yours, Mew! "

He came that afternoon. The same rugged sensitive figure, his voice of an even greater flexibility, eyes more deeply humorous, and hair just beginning to silver at the temples.

"Well, Mew, so you're married and have a son! Where is he? Let me see him. If he has been bad to-day I'll give him a penny, but if he has been good I'll give him a sound smacking. . . . So this is he," and he looked down at Paul Jr. standing by me on tiptoe with excitement at this incredibly wicked and anarchistic grown-up. "Well," — looking him over with an appraising eye — "here's a penny for you. Any day you've been really bad come to me and I'll give you another. Never mind your mother. She's like all American parents, doesn't know a thing about bringing up children. Only now beginning to learn the dictionary. For God's sake, don't let her fill you up on tea. Run along now and play with some matches, and if you can't find any, pick all the nice flowers in the window-boxes. There's a good boy."

When we were alone, we sat down and began to talk. We talked through tea, through whisky, through dinner. Through the night. Italian newspapers, American glaciers, English letters, sexual relations in Sicily, blood relations all over the world, music, Russian ballet (then in Paris), Russian emperors, more music, Nietzsche and back to English letters again. I spoke of a story I had seen by D. H. Lawrence in the *English Review,* called *Vin Ordinaire.* It was the first short story by Lawrence I had read and I was immensely impressed by its compactness, its emotional tensity and technical expertness.

"A fine talent D. H." said Douglas. "If he doesn't

break down. Devilish poor, you know, in bad health and all that. Needs help; in love with some woman, German, I believe . . . yes, they ' love ' each other so much they throw chairs at each other. If he isn't killed by one, it won't do him any harm. But he needs help. No English periodical pays you enough to buy ink with, and he needs something to tide him over for a bit, so if you liked the ſtory send some along. The time will come when he won't need it. But don't forget that he has written one of the good novels of our time, *Sons and Lovers.*" There is a play in which Coquelin Aîné used to aĉt where an old gentleman climbing down a mountainside slipped and would have fallen to his death had not a young man who was taking the same road reached out and saved him: and the old gentleman, overwhelmed with gratitude, begged the younger to make the reſt of the journey with him. As time progressed he found himself so irritated by the mounting debt of gratitude he owed, that he could not bear the sight of his saviour, and the journey ended in bitter enmity. Perhaps some impulse of this kind caused the spirited and fluent sparring which went on between D. H. Lawrence and Norman Douglas a few years ago, through the preface of *M.M.* and Douglas's answer in *Manners.* Perhaps it was something else again.

Douglas scolded me roundly for my fanatical admiration of Henry James, juſt for the sake of scolding, as in reality he held him to be a writer of considerable gifts. I pointed out that he knew all there was to know of American parents, which in itself should have endeared him to Douglas. When they met in my house, as they

To [?] from
N.

Jan 1928

NORMAN DOUGLAS

occasionally did, the conversation between them was of
the most desultory character. They were too fundamen-
tally divergent in their approach to life, and diametrically
opposed in matters of style and technique even to bring
about conflict between them, to say nothing of agreement.
After the salutary lecture he administered on the dangers
of becoming hypnotized by the sheer pleasure of process
to be derived from H. J., Douglas at last let me talk to
him about himself and his own writings, by then become
a structure immeasurably distant from " But Alberique
had fainted away." Working myself up into a frenzy of
excitement, I made him listen until dawn. As the light
began to cloud the clear blackness of the sky through the
glass over our heads, he rose from the depths of one of
the big armchairs and said:

" Ah well, my dear Mew, it's perfectly clear that I am
the only person left alive who can write the English
language and you the only person who can appreciate it.
Run along to bed now, and mind you start that boy of
yours off in the morning with a really sound thrashing.
He has been damned quiet to-night."

This was the first of many nights of cherished discussions. Startlingly disrespectful, was Douglas, of anything
but the best. Exceptional powers of destructive criticism,
Spartan standards of intellectual discipline and Baby-
lonian standards of moral tolerance made his conversation
stimulating and enlightening beyond that of most men
I have known. Humour ran the whole gamut from the
subtlest shades possible to be conveyed by a pause, to the
most solid salacious outbursts that can be expressed in

the splendid coarseness of the English language. Particularly adroit was he in the use of good old Anglo-Saxon words of one syllable. Servants were in a state of shocked adoration, even the miracle maids, imperturbable as they were, finding it at moments difficult to serve him in perfect solemnity. As for the Irish angel, she would snatch Paul Jr. into the safety to be found behind a locked nursery door, crossing herself as she flew upstairs with him the minute Douglas entered the house. But she would come down in an amazingly short time again on some perfectly needless errand or other, and hover about the premises, her face scarlet with embarrassed delight and murmuring, " Glory be to God, madame, he's *terrible*."

This would bring a chuckle from Douglas that was the most satisfactory sound one could hear. I did not tell you about that chuckle? It was focused in his throat, drawing into itself all the nourishment that could be extracted from every different part of the incomparably complex mechanism known as a human body. His eyes would send gleams of merriment through nearly closed eyelids, that became tears as they reached his throat. Ears would send the echo of everything they had heard in life, to add colour to the solid gurgling bulk of sound that centred there. Quivering nostrils sent shafts of shivering light that played on it. The throat itself became a cylindrical container to hold this phenomenon. Hands offered memories of tactile experience that touched it into constantly changing shapes. Lungs bellowed to keep it inflated with the breath to live and a heart pumped it full of blood. Food, good and bad, that had lived through his stomach (he has written somewhere that the man who cannot appreciate a good dinner on earth is not fitted to taste the joys offered him in heaven) strengthened the very body of this noise. Legs that had climbed mountains and wandered in valleys gave it rhythm, and the seed of his body that begot two sons gave it birth. Such was his chuckle. I crossed the ocean three years ago to hear it and came back refreshed. Standing in an English country lane, I have heard bells ringing out and up to a star-filled sky from a church tower of stone that have not done as much.

MUSIC AT MIDNIGHT

A Florentine Week
1913

So my life passed through the winter and spring of 1912 and 1913. At the end of the season Paul and I went to Florence for a brief visit with Mabel Dodge. Robin de la Condamine, who divided his life between London and Florence came along with us, and we took Arthur Rubinstein and John McMullin, — Mabel having told us to bring anyone we liked.

During a stray Paris week-end in Mrs. Webb's apartment (she had deserted the Capri scene for the more homelike atmosphere of the Avenue Henri Martin), I had found that unique Californian, John McMullin, and, liking him very much indeed, had simply insisted upon his returning to London with us at once; and, still liking him very much indeed, further insisted upon his joining our caravan to Florence.

In a procession of fiacres we arrived at the Villa Curonia late at night, pulling up the steep hill which it crowned. The midnight blackness was carved with the gallant cracking of whips over the backs of the indifferent sturdy little bastard Arabian horses who did the pulling. You could smell the iris and roses that grew at the foot of the cedar trees which lined the winding *viale* to the house: you could see the fluttering light of fireflies through the wheat that flourished under the olive groves at either side of it. You could only guess at the stars, so high the sky was that night. Axles screaming, coachmen swearing, little horses with broken wind heaving, we arrived at the villa to find it full of people, everyone a little cross at sitting up so late. Carl Van Vechten was there, playing *Scherherezade* a trifle sulkily on the piano. Robert Edmond Jones was there; indeed, he had wisely gone to bed. Jack Reed was there, pulling restless hands through curling hair in splendid impatience. Mary Foote was there, looking that exotic thing which she will not let herself be. And Mabel, of course, in the centre of it, sitting calmly. After the customary strange noises and odd antics with which friends greet each other, I insisted upon waking Robert E. Jones. Terribly irritating thing to do, but he was very nice about it, as I rushed into his big high bedroom hung in folds of red brocade, and shook him awake. He blinked sleep-soft brown eyes at me and then said, " I like your hat, and your earrings are perfect. I'll show you some stuffs and bits I bought to-day," and he leaped out of bed to a corner of the room, from which he returned with a basket full of brocades, velvets, delicately dilapidated fans of exquisite design and a few lovely stained lengths of linen. He showed them all to me in eager excitement and we immediately began discussing clothes, costumes, colours and rooms, until I was pulled away by less enthusiastic but more benevolent friends.

The week was interesting.

I cannot conceive of more conflicting psychological elements meeting under similar conditions without an

explosion. There was not one, but there was a constant
ferment. Mabel was installed on the second floor of the
villa with her original collection of guests, and I was
established on the ground floor with her additional ones I
had brought with me from London. Almost everyone was
in love or in hate, and only Mary Foote could come cutting through the snarled air like a cool smooth silver
fruit-knife, severing at the crucial moments the crossed
threads that were in danger of becoming firmly knotted
entanglements. It would afford a breathing space until
the throwing of spools of contention between the first
and second floors would begin again. The breakfast hour
was comparatively serene, as we all had it in our
rooms, or at least in the rooms of our choice. As the
morning grew to noon, different members of the household would begin wandering through the many large
and small rooms that honeycombed the villa. Enemies
of the night before could pass each other safely in the
big rooms, but in a small room of many doors it was
a precarious adventure. Friends would meet by assigna-
tion in what they had anticipated would be a deserted
gallery and find themselves unwelcome intruders in a
whispered conference. Mabel and I would always manage to exchange some signal of amity above the general
traffic, conveying the message that all was really not
quite what it seemed and would come out differently
in the end.

Of an evening Bobbie would ask me to pose for him
the next day in the same dress and headdress in which I
was that night savagely encased. I would agree. We

would meet in a small upstairs library, and Bobbie would begin a sketch. Just as he would have worked himself up to the point where he decided that my head feathers ought to be really six inches longer instead of just outrageously high as they were, " they must be more so, Muriel, more so — everything about you is *more* so. Your clothes should be even more *more* so," Carl would peer around a bookshelf, grey curls dancing over brown eyes standing still and grave. " Don't be ridiculous, Bobbie, she's strange enough looking as it is. She should dress very simply, in black, no headdress at all, no earrings, nothing but her own strange face, and nothing, I say, nothing else to distract your attention from it. Have you no sense of dramatic values at all? You'll never make a success of the stage if you go on this way."

" Carl, I am not discussing it with you. We have discussed it all before, and I refuse to say another word to you about it. I am not drawing you."

" But you will discuss it," Carl would shriek. " Your future depends on it."

And they did discuss it. In the meanwhile I would be left standing there, wishing to God I had stayed in bed and noting how appallingly unbecoming a long lemon yellow dress, with a short tight bright blue bodice embroidered with scarlet, pink and magenta beads, can be at ten o'clock in the morning, particularly when finished off by a turban of all the colours together, adorned by a flaming osprey in the centre.

Jack Reed, alarmed by the loud voices in which the altercation between Carl and Bobbie was by now pitched, would appear suddenly, standing nervously still but ready to move powerfully.

" Carl, stop it, or you'll cry! " he would shout.

I was the one really ready to cry so I would turn to Jack with a prayer for deliverance. He would lead me gently but firmly out of the room, down to the first floor and into my bedroom. " If you changed those clothes, perhaps, Muriel, you know . . . if you just changed those clothes." Then *I* would lose my temper.

" Why should I? It is a divine dress and the turban took me ten minutes to wind round my head. I don't want to change them. In fact, I *won't*. I shall keep them on all day, and if we must go to the Braggiottis to lunch I'll wear them there. Why do you object to them? I suppose you are thinking of the poor devils who have sweated to make them. Well, I don't care if they have. If they could wear them they wouldn't have to make them — there is a chemistry about things that is much more important than justice and . . ."

" Now, stop it, Muriel. Stop it. You're talking like a fool. Stop it at once." Ultimately I would quiet down.

Always I see Jack Reed stopping things to make room for life to be lived in.

John McMullin would then peer in at my bedroom door in perfect pyjamas and dressing-gown, and say very sleepily and a little crossly, " Mools darling, what are you making such a row about at this hour in the morning? I have not been able to sleep a wink. Don't you ever stop talking? Undress and go to bed. What time is it? "

" Time for lunch! I have been to bed. Hurry and get dressed and don't scold me. I am unhappy."

Lunch, as you can well imagine under those circumstances, was not an easy meal. Arthur Rubinstein and Paul would come in late from playing and singing some new Sczymanowski songs. As his songs are incomparably difficult, these two would stand up for minutes by the chairs we were waiting for them to sit down in, and dispute a musical interval. Arthur's voice was in the category of composers' voices, but his musical memory was unimpeachable, and he could sing very loud. He was usually right, and Draper would finally sit down, amicably defeated, and begin his belated spaghetti. Arthur would hum in unquenchable musical enthusiasm as he ate. This would be the crowning touch for Mabel, who up to that time had sat smilingly silent. She could move with swift direction when she wanted to, and at lunch she often wanted to. With instructions to a servant to the effect that he should inform the *Villa Braggiotti* that the *Villa Curonia* regretted that they could not come to lunch (it would then be two o'clock in the afternoon) she would order the car, walk out of the room into it and go to Bologna. Small wonder, poor dear, turned out of her own house.

An afternoon of sleep would pacify us, and dinner had even chances of success. Of course, Carl did not care for Bach, and Arthur played it as often as I asked him to, which was every night.

It was on one of these nights that Mabel asked the frail tailored Englishwoman and her blue-caped attendant nurse to dine — the same nurse who had, on a previous occasion in the Villa Curonia, made such valiant attempts to free Beethoven from the restraining pink satin ribbons that held him to the piano. They came every year to Florence, these two, and as it had been suggested by a discreet few (or were they tactful?) that the troubled nights at the villa might be attributed to ghostly manifestations, of which the villa was never quite free, the idea of asking the mediumistic little nurse and her mistress to investigate such possibilities seemed a good one. They arrived. The English lady had the worn features of a delicate, rather dissipated young man, and the charm of one, as she walked quickly across the loggia to greet Mabel, swinging her inevitable slender walking-stick by her side. From the obscure shadow behind her stepped the prim, starched figure of the nurse. She wore the same long blue cape and, between its folds, a heavy gold cross was just visible on her breast; on her head she wore the small bonnet-like hat of her profession. Her prominent, bulging eyes showed sightlessly behind the strong magnifying glass of her gold-rimmed spectacles.

The heat of the day had been intense, and still hovered in the arches of the loggia. We sat in nervous listlessness until dinner was announced. The cool, high walls of the dining-room refreshed us. For once, we could discuss a subject about which there could be no finality of opinion, and which was yet sufficiently interesting — ghosts. We recounted the various fragmentary tales we had heard and experiences we probably had not had. The English lady contributed some very lively ones of her own. The dead were as real and simple a part of her life as the living. The nurse kept a timid, formal silence, broken only with a " Yes, indeed it was so," " No, indeed there was not," or a " Quite right, indeed," when her diſtinguished patient turned to her for verification or correction. She was perfeCtly at home in all queſtions concerning the names, clothes, habits and characters assumed by inhabitants of other worlds.

I queſtioned Mabel about a particular wall between two rooms, across which diſturbed lighted shadows had been seen to wander through a pattern of small flames, to the considerable discomfort of the occupants of both rooms. A sober old cook of the Villa Curonia had slept in one of them for a time, until she aroused and terrified the household with piercing shrieks that brought them all to her door. They arrived in time to see her burſt through it, crossing herself, and sobbing with fright as she moaned her tale of a " spirit like a prieſt, lighting candles on a wall to say Mass." She was not to be induced, by threat or command, into reëntering the room, and in a courageous persiſtence of refusal she had hobbled away down a darkened passage, and out of sight.

Some time after this, a professor of sorts, less fancifully inclined, had slept a night or two in the room the other side of the wall, and had not seemed convinced by his own report of a sleepless night, due to fireflies flitting slowly across the side of his room. In the central upſtairs hall, from which one entered all the bedrooms, copper bowls had been seen to dance about on a table in an agitation that, with the beſt will in the world, was difficult to explain by the vibration of passing feet. In a small cell of a bedroom on the ground floor, sheets and blankets that covered the most virtuous of sleepers would be unaccountably snatched to the floor . . . and so it went on.

Carl was getting a little hysterical: Bobbie was dramatically aroused: even Jack Reed listened. Mary Foote and Paul decided that a ride in a Fifth Avenue 'bus would do us all good, but, alas, time and space interposed certain difficulties. Only the little nurse remained outwardly unmoved. She sat in trance-like stolidity.

The last cup of coffee was drunk. Mabel rose from her chair at the head of the table, and we followed her out of the dining-room, and on to the loggia. Change of surroundings brought a relaxation of the tension so fictitiously aroused by haphazard surmisings, vaguely defined " scientific " explanations and wishful theories. Only the little figure under the blue cape became more concentrated. One could not ignore her. Her very silence was increasingly oppressive.

Finally, the invalided lady from England rose to go. In spite of her charm, we all rose with eager relief and began a straggling movement through the vast rooms of the villa toward the front door. The nurse moved stiffly in her shadow, eyes in a tepid glaze of sightlessness.

Suddenly, in the centre of the splendid empty courtyard which one crossed to reach the entrance to the villa, the diminutive figure under the blue cape ceased to move. . . . After what seemed an interminable moment, she lifted her head slightly, as if listening for some sound. We stood still to watch her. Her mistress spoke:

"Come on, my dear; don't ſtand there all night."

As her eyes did not see, so her ears did not hear. For another moment she ſtood thus, and then, with unhuman swiftness, she moved through the air, and up a small rarely-used ſtone ſtaircase that was ſteeply built up from a corner of the court. We followed. Who would have dared ſtay behind?

She paused a moment at the top of the ſtaircase, then turned abruptly and moved forward with the same un-natural swiftness in the direction of the two troubled rooms. In the hallway that led to them she ſtopped by the table on which the copper bowls were placed, and began to speak in a low whisper. As we liſtened, the words grew more and more diſtinct.

"Yes, yes," excitedly, "yes, yes, your Worship; I hear you — yes. . . ." She fingered the heavy gold cross under her cape. "Yes!" the voice went on. "I will help you. I underſtand." She was speaking in very low but firm tones now. "I will follow you if you will show me the way. Yes, your Worship — show me."

She ſtood aside as if to let someone pass, and then dropped quickly on one knee, her eyes, through their gold-rimmed spectacles, ſtrained upward in reverent awe. Rising, she ſtarted forward again, as if answering a beck-oning geſture, and walked quickly paſt us down the hall. We moved after her, mere shadowy elusive wraiths, re-lentlessly urged to the pursuit of this curiously real queſt, known only to the figure who was leading us.

Before the door of the room in which the eminent pro-fessor had found no reſt, she ſtopped to turn the handle of

the door, and then unhesitatingly stepped into the room.
Turning to the wall where glimmering lights had darkened the understanding of cook and scholar alike, again
she dropped on one knee and made the sign of the cross.
Then, rising to her feet, she stood listening. Suddenly, in
a voice that shook with anger and indignation, she cried
out:

" It is an outrage, your Worship, an outrage — to have
it stolen from you while you were saying Mass! The
scoundrel! The *thief!* " her voice gradually rising until
the last word was a shriek. " I will find him, your Honour; I will find him, and I will return it to you — for it
was stolen, I tell you! " Then, lowering her voice, she
continued in subdued tones, soothingly: " You shall rest
this night easily in your bed, your Honour, for the crucifix
will be found."

She sprang out of the room and past us. From the hall
where we had stood rooted to the floor in frozen fear,
we watched her as she rushed like a mad thing in and out
of bedrooms, her long blue cape flying behind her, scolding under her breath from time to time. " The scoundrel!
The thief! He *stole* it. . . . The poor, blessed father,
wandering and hunting . . ." She was whispering
again, " But I will find it; yes, yes — I will find it."

She hurried out of the last room, staring eyes fixed,
rushed down the stairs, through the courtyard and down
a dark narrow corridor which led to the room where even
the innocent sleeper had been molested. At its open door
she stopped, every line of her rigid little body brittle with
defiant antagonism, a look of sly caution creeping over

her face, and even invading the eyes. Then she leapt across the threshold into the room. She stood there with hands clenched, words coming very fast from her dry lips:

" So it's you, is it? " she shouted. " I've caught you at last, you thieving scoundrel! Sneaking in and out of other people's rooms — pulling things about to see what you can find. It's stealing, that is what it is — stealing, and you are a thief, in spite of your cowl. . . . And it is the Father's ivory and gold crucifix you have in your hand this very minute, you wicked monk! "

She shook her bony fists in the face of her imaginary foe, her hard-worked knuckles showing white through the red roughened skin, a stain of yellow acid on her bent thumb. Then, as if avoiding a blow, she jerked her head swiftly to one side. After a short second of controlled suspense, she clutched at something in the air before her. Turning with a look of triumph that glorified the plain little features, she gasped, " I have it! " and flung herself through the doorway down the corridor she had traversed so surely a moment before, and across the courtyard one last time, with hands outstretched.

As she reached the foot of the stairs in her eager journey to restore the crucifix to its ever-seeking owner, she fell in a huddled heap on the stone floor, lying motionless under the folds of the blue cape.

. . . .

Hours later, a shrill, dolorous cry broke the unlighted silence into which the villa had sunk. It was the white peacock, calling to its mate, who was given to flying

Paul Draper, Sr., and Paul Draper, Jr. Steyning, Sussex, England, 1913

wantonly over the wall into the wooded vale below,
where the nightingales sang. . . . Or was it?

As a tribute to Mrs. Stanford White, I uncrossed my
fingers, but was not answered.

It was the crowning touch of that visit.

One week was enough. We all parted and went our
different ways. Mabel and I plotted to see each other
somewhere soon (we had hardly exchanged a word) and
the procession of fiacres and sturdy diminutive Arabian
steeds took us down the hill again to the trains . . . and
on to Vienna and Paris and back to London once more.
The last thing I heard was Carl's voice, as he pointed
to the head of one of the horses up from which a feather
duster about five feet high sprang into the air and down
from which hung bells, red tassels and leather straps,
saying derisively, " There, Bobbie, that's what you want
Muriel to look like! "

I do, rather.

. . . .

London was pleasantly calm for the few days we spent
in Edith Grove before packing up for Steyning, where
we went for the third summer of study. So much work
had been accomplished by Draper in the intervening year
that the lessons were more in the nature of a preparation
of concert programs than technical work. We had a tiny
farmhouse of our own that year, with a farmer and his
wife to look after us and it, which was ideal. It cost us
two and sixpence a week. It was close to Wiston Old
Rectory, and Mühlen brought us armfuls of flowers and
vegetables from his garden every day or two. His garden

and his doves were his only recreation in the country, and strawberries and cream his only indulgence. Many other pupils were dotted about the countryside. John McMullin (he was not a pupil) took another of those small farmhouses in the near neighbourhood, and we sank down exhausted after our Florentine holiday. Is it Walter Pater who speaks of Florence during the Renaissance as a " city of secret sin and exquisite amusement " ? During one week of July in the year 1913 it was neither.

MUSIC AT MIDNIGHT

Edith Grove
1913-1914

THE PROSPECTS FOR 1913–14 in Edith Grove were good. The Russian Ballet were planning a six weeks' season at Drury Lane, and the Covent Garden Opera programs included Mozart's *Magic Flute* and Strauss' *Rosenkavalier,* to say nothing of Beethoven's *Fidelio* which for all its dreary passages (there even Paul agreed with me) has moments of unsurpassed musical purity. Casals and Thibaud were to play the Brahms double concerto with Sir Henry Wood's orchestra, Kochanski was to play Sczymanowski's violin concerto a few days after Paul's projected concert of his songs. Karol would be there himself and Rubinstein was to accompany Paul in the Sczymanowski songs. By Christmas there would be two sons. It looked as if 19 and 19A Edith Grove needed expansion. The departure of the music-loving old lawyer from number 17 left a vacant house adjoining 19, and so we took it. I began knocking walls down again and, when we moved up from Steyning, we could overflow into three houses instead of two. A little weary from supervising plasterers, "arranging" about fire laws with insurance agents and fitting out nurseries (I am not very good on nurseries) I took the first part of the concert season quietly. Took it gently, as dear Henry James had cautioned Montague Vert Chester to take his meeting with him. Our first evening was inaugurated by the playing of the Mendelssohn and Schubert octets and the Schubert quintet for two celli and the Beethoven B flat quartet, a program which had become almost a ritual at Edith Grove.

The London String Quartet, led by Albert Sammons, was composed of Waldo Warner as second violinist, Petrie as viola, and Warwick Evans as cellist. They had come to Edith Grove toward the end of the previous season, when their position in London as the first string quartet of that city was unchallenged. I do not believe it has been challenged since, though Sammons is no longer leader. I have not heard it for years. In 1913 it was a balanced combination of talents, creating an ensemble that was of perfectly unified variety. Sammons, a violinist gifted in high degree, could have had a career as a solo violinist (he played the Beethoven violin concerto and Sir Edward Elgar's concerto with orchestra during the season) on his own. He preferred the quartet, to their advantage. After the B flat Beethoven quartet, Warwick Evans grumbling and growling over a pretended disinterest for the work, an attitude which he couldn't maintain under the spell it cast over him in the execution of it, they played as a reward for him the Debussy string quartet in an unforgettable performance. With *L'Après-Midi d'un Faune* and *Pelléas et Mélisande,* the string quartet makes the third masterpiece of that composer's musical output.

Rubio, in honour of the inauguration of the 1913–14 season at Edith Grove, brought an enormous canvas to

hang over the mantelpiece. I had found a fragment of
Gothic tapestry that was just right for that place and it
had been hanging there for a year to everyone's satisfac-
tion. But Rubio's enthusiasm for his masterpiece was
so genuine, it afforded him such real pleasure to
make a sacrifice of it for the adornment and aggran-
dizement of our brick walls, that there was no refusing
it — at least for the time being. It depicted a very
over-developed young boy with freshly painted pink
cheeks and belladonna-d brown eyes, wrapped in a
faithful spot-to-spot reproduction of a leopard skin. He
was seated on a rock, clinging firmly to a stout and
rather chic cane, of a chic that pervades the shops of
Neapolitan arcades. To Rubio it was a " veritable Rubens, veritable! " and was a portrait of St. John the Bap-
tist. Despite inner misgivings, the tapestry came down
and the " Rubens " went up, Rubio supervising the en-
terprise with tender solicitude. When it was accomplished
and the picture in place, he stood in the middle of the
floor beaming with benevolence and pride, first at us and
then at the cherished Rubens. Finally he turned to Paul
and myself, his eyes moist, and said, with a wave of the
hand in the direction of the portrait:

" *Dunque, mes chères* children, *vous ne pouvez pas
avere qualche cosa di piu* magnifi*cent!* " Nor could we.
No royal grant was ever more graciously bestowed, no
personal deprivation so nobly suffered. It must have cost
him his heart's blood. Tapestry or no tapestry, it was
decreed that as long as the walls stood and we lived between them the veritable Rubens should remain. A for-

tuitous accident to do with a smoking chimney solved the difficulty some months later. The canvas was darkening perceptibly under the constant thick clouds of smoke that issued from the fireplace beneath it, and it was decided, after serious conferences on the subject, that it must be removed. Rubio was desolate, but a Rubens was a Rubens and great masterpieces belonged to the future. Reluctantly he received it once more into the safety of his own four smokeless walls, fearful of having hurt our feelings. May someone like him be somewhere about in heaven to give me a hand if I ever get near enough to reach it.

On the night he went with us to hear the Brahms double concerto played by his beloved " Pablissimo " and Thibaud, Sir Claude Phillips, that artful critic of good pictures and all good things of life, having heard the tale of the " veritable Rubens," greeted him with the respect due a connoisseur and entered into serious conversation with him on the subject of painting in general and Rubens in particular. As he talked, he scratched the tip of his biggish pink nose with a twisted little finger, a trick very characteristic of him and inimitably recorded for all time in a caricature of him drawn by Max Beerbohm and currently exhibited at Leicester Galleries, portraying him in the very act of confiding to a fellow critic that he found Max's exhibition in " execrable taste this year — execrable! " Henry James described it, cruelly enough, as the gesture of an old woman with cold cream on her nose trying to scratch one tiny tickling point on it without smudging the cold cream. His cherubic countenance, framed in scant sandy blond locks, was a familiar one at Edith Grove and very welcome. He was an inspired listener of music and, in spite of being a great chatterer, was never heard to whisper during a performance. After Casals' concert he and Lady Cunard came back to Edith Grove with us and listened to Sammons and his three brothers-in-music as they lilted through a Haydn quartet, while waiting for Thibaud and Casals to join us. " Couldn't we play the Borodin just once before they get here? " moaned Warwick Evans; " otherwise I'm afraid you'll want another Haydn."

" How about some Mozart — that is if Mozart has written any chamber music," queried Lady Cunard.

" If he'd written any more he'd have bust his —— "

" There, there, Warwick," I interjected, " never mind. He didn't write any more than he did after all. He — er — he — er only wrote — er as many as he *did* write, you know, and Lady Cunard only wanted to know — er — er — Let's go to supper."

A very extraordinary woman, Lady Cunard. As Maud Alice Burke from New York, she arrived in England, and married Sir Bache Cunard, who used to beat gold into small fantastic shapes in a room at the top of the house, while she beat certain sections of London society into shape and drove it ahead of her with determination and success. Intelligent, astute, untiring and powerful, she used all these qualities to make London a more amusing (definitely pre-war word) place to live in. Centuries of tradition had already given it the shapeliness that life assumes when based on class distinction without class separation. London was, indeed, one of the perfect cities to live in during the epochal era that disappeared from the face of the world in August 1914. In no capital of Europe could prime ministers be made so easily at dinner-tables, yet perhaps in no capital of Europe could dinner-tables become so small. The engagement of Russian dancers was discussed with due solemnity in the galleries of the House of Parliament, and M. P.'s clamoured for boxes when the engagement thus settled was due to open. Lady Cunard was a colourful thread running through this weaving and could manage Lloyd George on one side and Nijinsky on the other with a dexterity of purpose that was pretty to watch. Without her able impresarioship, I doubt if we would have had Diaghilev and his ballet for that memorable season in London. And for that alone, one is devoutly thankful. Mozart, fortunately, is safely beyond the necessitous calculations of patronage and one auditor more or less does not jeopardize his supremacy. The most likable thing about Lady Cunard was her alert eagerness and zest for new things, an enlivening counterfoil to the superb indifference and imperturbable style, in its truest sense, with which life in London was lived. I feel sure that when she discovered the Mozart quartets she was as excited and interested as she was upon hearing Stravinsky's *Sacre du Printemps* for the first time. New experiences both, and therefore equally important. No pretence about her.

· · · · · · · · ·

When Thibaud and Casals finally arrived that night, Thibaud was dropping with fatigue. We sent him down to the studio for a nap on one of the big floor cushions until he should feel refreshed enough to join us. Going back to the studio after supper, we found him stretched out sound asleep before the fire. Our entrance failed to arouse him. So did an hour or two of music. People left fairly early that night, until only a handful remained. There was a question of morning boat-trains to catch in order to fulfil an engagement in Paris the next evening, and Chester was getting worried about the depths of sleep in which Thibaud lay as one buried. As I was protesting against his intention of waking him, Thibaud abruptly sprang from the cushion straight up into the air like a suddenly sprouting tree, and very wide awake.

" I will play the Bach *Chaconne,*" he announced.

He crossed the room, took his marvellous fiddle out of its case, and standing over by the Goddess of Charity under flowers of Burmese gold, a little sheltered by the folds of the screen, he played the Bach *Chaconne*. No one violinist of my hearing has ever touched the heights of this work that Thibaud reached that night. Perhaps he himself could never repeat it. He placed it surely and beautifully before us. He showed us every integral part of that greatly builded structure, and from its summit flung out its full emotional content, with a technique that created itself to meet the demands of his performance. To play once like that in a lifetime is enough. His small privileged audience found itself on its feet when he brought it to its close, and at the top of the stairs stood Paul Jr., red-gold hair standing up on his head, eyes swimming with blue waters of sleep from which he had emerged, cheeks blazing pink from excitement, clad in a bright green dressing-gown. No one spoke and he came down into the room saying, " I've come because I heard such beautiful music."

Thibaud caught him up in his arms and leapt up the stairs to the dining-room with him. We did not follow them, but some half hour later found them there, feeding each other dilapidated bits of food and making dangerous experiments with the coffee-machine. . . . Years afterward, when I could bring myself to speak to Thibaud of that night's playing of the Bach *Chaconne,* he said simply:

" *Oui, j'ai bien joué çe soir-la.*"

. . . .

In December of 1913 my second son was born and when he was three days old he went to his first party. I was carried downstairs and installed on the big sofa, and I tucked him under my arm in a corner of it where he lay quite peaceably, waking and sleeping at his leisure and supping when he was hungry. This particularly pleased Casals, whose reverence for birth and children mounted to a passion almost tribal in its intensity. It outraged the admirable but conventional little English nurse who was taking care of us both, and she was quite ready to agree with Douglas about American parents, though from a different angle. They played a Brahms sextet, my beloved Schubert quintet, and Warwick Evans even offered to play the Beethoven C# Minor

PAUL JR., WITH "BUTTONS *Jetté-d*, AS IT WERE, JUST THERE!"

quartet. Such lavish gifts to lay at the feet of a three-days-old child! Casals played a Bach suite and Arthur Rubinstein the Chopin B flat sonata and some Scriabin. Everyone was looking forward to the engagement of Diaghilev's Ballet, announced for May, June and July of '14, and Chaliapin's promised coöperation in Russian operas. Stravinsky's *Sacre* and its astounding première in Paris was much discussed. Casals was glowing with excitement over his recaptured romance with Susan Metcalf, whom he subsequently married, and though he was making brave efforts to keep it secret, manifested it in every gesture, word and expression, so that at last I said, " I know everything about it but the name, Pablissimo, and I can divine that."

" What are you talking about? Everything about what? " with an attempt at bewilderment.

" Why, the state you're in. Could it be Miss Metcalf? You spoke of her once to me in Holland Street and you let your cigar burn your finger as you talked. For a cellist, that bespeaks an absorption that is not to be lightly dismissed. Please tell me it is she."

" You are a devil," he answered, very tenderly, and would say no more.

Paul sang *Lord Rendel My Son* with a dramatic fervor which never broke through the austere control with which he directed it, and followed it with *Kläge* by Brahms, one of the loveliest and most poignant of his songs. His singing this year was at its best. The Sczymanowski concert, with a program of German, English, French and Russian songs, had been seriously and enthusiastically received. There were plans afoot to go to Germany after the London season and sing the *Winterreise* cycle of Schumann to German audiences.

.   .   .   .

In May, 1914, the Russian Ballet arrived and great was the excitement thereof. Sir Thomas Beecham was one of the guarantors who was to conduct one or two performances, and Pierre Monteux, a French conductor of great intelligence and musicianship, was to conduct the rest. To digress for a moment, it is unfortunate that Monteux did not succeed in gaining the recognition in this country which is due him as one of the truly gifted and significant orchestra conductors we have to-day. He builds programs with unusually judicious selectivity; he pulls a tone-texture of great depth and richness out of the men playing under him; he knows the music-literature of all countries.

To go back to Diaghilev and the Russian Ballet. They came and all of London turned out to greet them. One of the most brilliant first-night audiences sat in row upon row upon row and in box after box after box. The program, if I remember correctly, was composed of *Scheherazade, Les Sylphides* and *Petrouchka*. Dancing that was new, fresh development of an old technique that wrote another chapter for itself, costumes and scenery that revolutionized the stage, and music that was based on unaccustomed tonalities set London in an uproar. Diaghilev was the permeating genius who was behind it, through it, around it and before it: responsible in undefinable ways (as well as those that are definably

144

within the province of a director) for every gesture, light
and shade, and measure of tempo. Of all the great artists
he has trained, what one ever achieved without him that
which was possible with him? Bakst, who designed much
of the scenery and costuming, has simply fallen into
oblivion since, and is recalled to our memory more often
by the horrible crudities of his imitators, or the chance
happy effect of his colour schemes on manufacturers of
felt hats and cotton dresses and woollen sweaters, than
by any fresh creation from his own brain. An occasional
exhibition gives evidence that now and again he does
something almost as good but never better. The fate of
Nijinsky is too tragic to dwell upon, poor witless retro-
gression of the human species that he has become. But
even before this, his sporadic attempts to organize his own
troupe and arrange his own season have repeatedly been
proved a failure. Karsavina, that exquisite embodiment
of musical and aesthetically right grace, is married
and mothering, but not dancing. The greatest dis-
tinctions of *Les Six,* that half dozen of intelligent
musical investigators and compilers of rhythm and sound,
have been in the works written for his productions, Lo-
pokova has married Maynard Keynes, the English econ-
omist, and dances agreeably enough at a party now and
then when the spirit moves her. And so it goes.

Diaghilev himself is a shade worn and tired now. The
years between 1914 and 1918 were as parlous for him and
his beloved dancers as they were for most. Music and
ballet on the grand scale are no more. Abortive democratic
principles, the socialization of the arts for the standardized

benefit of the prolific " brotherhood " of man, the lack
of one great figure to dominate so many interrelated parts
of the world as have been thrown pell-mell together, all
these currents have accelerated the temporary eclipse of
the grand scale. No conscious nobility of purpose in life
and therefore no great living. No great living, and therefore less and less great art. They are losing the code, and
with a universal increase of intelligence and technical virtuosity that is in almost exact inverse ratio to standards
of value, there is little left that can be presented on the
grand scale. What there is of it Diaghilev captures and
salvages. I have sat with him in almost empty theatres
during rehearsal and heard him say to the chef d'orchestra, very politely,

" *Non, non, non, maître. Pas tout à fait ça . . . Pas
tout à fait ça. Est-ce que je me trompe, ou est-ce que ce
n'est pas un tout petit trop . . . trop lent? En tout
cas, essayons-le un to-o-out petit peu plus vite. C'est bien
possible que j'ai tort.*" Or to a dancing figure on the
stage, " *Non, non, non, ma chère petite. Non. L'estomac
n'est pas fait du bois, — attendez, attendez, écoutez-moi
— ni de caoutchouc. Non, chère, non. L'estomac est fait
de la chair, après tout, de la bonne chair.*" And so on
and so on until by a series of almost chemical emanations
rather than actual directions, he had changed the atomic
structure of bodies, scenes and sounds.

I once asked him if he could express in words the exact
thing of which he was possessed that brought about this
subtle synthesis of flesh and light and tone vibration.

" *Je ne sais pas, je ne sais pas, ma chère Muriel. Je ne*

*sais pas. Un toooout petit peu de la connaissance peut-être,
et beaucoup de l'amour. . . . Je ne sais pas."*

The season was an overwhelming success. Lady
Cunard had the question of boxes and who should sit in
them well in hand, and rose triumphantly over feuds and
furies with her alert blond head darting from one box
to another and her intelligent little face everywhere.
Richard Strauss came to conduct his own Ballet *La
Legende de Joseph,* which, in spite of all Diaghilev
could do for it, was a lifeless work built on common-
place themes and feeble climaxes. He was staying with
the then Sir Edgar and Lady Speyer, who had a grand
party for him. Their magnificent establishment was ad-
mirably planned. Though hundreds could move freely
through the rooms, in spite of innumerable priceless
objects of furniture with which they were filled, she
seldom had more than a few really delightful people at
a time. An excellent musician and zealous violinist, she
had a flair for parties, and would hire the whole London
Symphony Orchestra for an evening to accompany
one artist, and ask twenty people to listen to it. There
were more than twenty asked to meet Sir Richard,
somewhat morose and lonely man that he seemed, but
everyone had a chance to talk to him and a chair to sit
down in.

The première of the *Sacre du Printemps* was imminent. Not a seat was procurable in the house for weeks
in advance. Rubinstein and Karol Sczymanowski were
staying with us at 17 Edith Grove, which I had broken
into and annexed, and Paul and Sozia Kochanski were

living in a charming little house across the street, so that no time should be lost getting from one end of London to the other. We started out together for the performances and stopped in at Covent Garden to hear *The Magic Flute*. We left in time to arrive at Drury Lane before the first note of *Sacre* began and found our way to our box through seething crowds of almost hysterically expectant people. The lights went down and, after a nervous silence in the darkness, Evan Evans came out on the curtained stage and tried to calm us with a nicely prepared, erudite little speech on the virtues and methods of the work we were about to hear. No one listened to him, though no one spoke. Just a ferment of restless rustling and dry coughing could be heard through the house in the darkness, like a many-tentacled, invisible, but omnipresent monster. Evan Evans hurriedly faltered into silence and bowed himself off stage. Monteux wormed his quiet way through the orchestra and stood tensely still for a full moment, an almost unbearable moment . . . and it began.

The score is part of musical history now, and the ballet is part of the history of the stage, so I will not analyze it from either point of view. I believe it to be one of the few great symphonic works of our time, and the ballet a most amazing visualization of the score. Nijinsky had the entire direction of it, with Diaghilev to turn to, and though he did not dance in it, it remains one of his unsurpassed achievements. Monteux extracted the full musical value the score contained, manipulated the complex and crashing rhythms of the final climax with uncanny clarity and coherence, filling the air with a sound that is still sinking down through me with every blood-beat. The house broke loose. The intensity of the score, which builds itself around and in you with each succeeding note and rhythm, leaving you no escape from its passionate logic, drove the audience to a pitch of frenzy. The sight of human beings moving in an abstract geometric design that became a symbol of eternal emotions, beyond-human in its effect, increased the force with which the music invaded you. When it ceased, people broke and ran, sat motionless and unapproachable, cried with rage and as-saulted sensibilities (" You call that *art,* do you? " " You call it *music? *" " My God! "), rushed to the bar for a drink or tried to laugh it away. They stumbled over seats, began clapping again in small groups, could not leave the theatre, could not go anywhere else. Many were shaken out of any capacity to form an opinion, provided they ever had any, and certainly were unable to pass judgment on a work so completely unrelated to habits of thinking and feeling already formed for them by time — that solid delusion, and environment, that erratic master.

I sat still in my chair until I could go out alone, and told the others I would meet them at Scott's Lobster House, the most neutral spot I could think of in which to talk without bursting with excitement. Edith Grove would have been too much for me that night. I was in a deadly calm at the moment but knew I would have to explode somewhere. My devotion to Bach, Brahms, Schu-bert and Beethoven, is not an attachment to those particular personal expressions of music to the exclusion of others. It is founded on the belief that there is no progression to eternity, only a different approach through varying ways and means, governed by chronological accidents of the periods of civilization which give it life. It was this approach in terms of music that engaged my adherence and interest, whether written to-day, to-morrow, or a thousand years ago. For me the stream had been freshly tapped. It is common talk now amongst amateurs and critics of music that *Sacre* is not, after the third or fourth or tenth hearing, so impressive. To those I would say, wait another fifteen years and hear it again without fear of remembering the mistake you might have made of over- or under-rating it in the first instance, and then you can really listen and judge once more.

We met at Scott's and, all talking at once, discussed until the early hours. Even Draper, who was reluctant to relinquish musical opinions and standards held since early childhood and whose tendency was to that form of exclusive adherence already indicated, was thrilled and forced to admit that here was something.

. . . .

And so the season of 1914 progressed from triumph to triumph. Chaliapin, in the rôles of Boris and Prince Igor, was at the top notch of his powers and was flinging one splendid performance after another at the feet of his adoring London audiences, who showered him with every attention in return. He came to Edith Grove shortly after the season began. His presence animated the rooms

like some elemental force. He had the shape and sub-
stance of a rock, the smell and sound of vast stretches of
earth and water, and breathed like the winds in the air.
I could never talk to him in that ceaseless word currency
we use with one another in ordinary parlance. I could
only look glad to see him, feel deeply at hearing him,
and salute him with a wave of the hand, a pat on the
shoulder, or a smile. He seldom used any other means
of communication, and we never misunderstood each
other. Very slow of speech, with irradiating smile,
pleasant blue eyes and pale yellow hair, powerfully tall
and lithely broad, he was a superb figure in those days.
When he laughed it rang under the dome of his opened
mouth and filled the room with its reverberations. The
same elemental power pervaded his music, and he was the
only person who was allowed to sit beside whoever was
playing the piano in chamber music *ensemble* at Edith
Grove, and hum the themes as he read them. This is the
most irritating thing that even a good musician can do, as
the sound of the human voice has too subjective a quality
to be absorbed in the delicate spare strength of a few essential instruments; but Chaliapin became one, and with
unerring pitch, could follow the thematic development
through every movement with a sound that was like
a new and hitherto unused instrument, a cunning combination of vibrations and percussions. He adored Arthur
Rubinstein and the field of chamber music being rela-
tively unfamiliar to his ear, it gave him intense pleasure
to watch it unfold under his eyes, so to speak. Grand
man!

Gertrude Stein was in London that year, and could be seen at most of the Drury Lane performances, stalking through crowds, adorned in a short corduroy skirt, a white silk shirt, sandals, and a tiny hat perched up on her monumental head. She was usually shadowed by a friend who was always draped in some semi-Oriental gauze of sorts, with clinking bracelets, tinkling chains and earrings as big and oval as her gaunt eyes. A strange pair. They came to Edith Grove, where Gertrude would sit in Buddhistic calm until some topic of conversation arose which stimulated her interests. And then she would talk for hours, a steady flow of ideas in an almost boring logical sequence, some of them profound and others merely a form of brilliant dialectic. Her point once gained or, in any case, her opponent once retired, she would sink back into calm and absorb intuitively what no longer aroused her intellectually. She was fascinated by my turbans and could give an accurate description of one, seen from as far away as an upper theatre-balcony, that would be complete in every detail, even to the setting of a stone that would dangle from it between my eyes. Is that eyesight or something else again?

She was sensitive about attacks upon her own peculiar form of literary expression, at least sensitive to any expressed or felt doubt of her sincerity. The technical aspect of it she would debate for hours, but her motive for developing it she would protect to the last drop of her mind's blood. She would say abruptly: " I don't know anything about it. I take things in and they come out that way, independent of conscious process. I don't know

GERTRUDE STEIN
"BEING MONUMENTAL IN A FIELD" (1928)

anything about it." She said she could not " do " a portrait of me because I " swooped so " she could not keep me still long enough. She wrote me a letter about myself a year ago, though, that kept me still long enough, I can tell you. I like her. I like her very much and agree with Sherwood Anderson that she " may be, just *may* be, the greatest word-slinger of our generation." Certainly she tried to break up word habits that no longer convey any meaning, so long have they been used as symbols of things that do not exist, and so often have they been dipped in and out of the pools of imagined and actual experience that lie deep in the history of the race. I wish she would break up mine. Look at that sentence for instance. It does not mean a thing.

Paul was infuriated by her writing, though personally devoted to her, and many a night was spent in bitter wrangling with him as to why a person is or is not entitled to use the word chair to convey whatever it may mean to that person, regardless of whether someone else conceives of it as an article of furniture to sit on or not. " But, Muriel, don't be ridiculous! You can't call anything else but a chair a chair," he would cry out in despair, as the dawn appeared at the windows.

" Why, certainly you can," I would answer. " It probably meant something quite different when it was first articulated, and is tired of being used to denote a silly stationary inanimate thing on four legs with a back to support our spinelessness. It probably wants to mean something else, to Gertrude anyway. Can't a word have a good time all by itself now and again? "

153

"Muriel, you're mad," Draper would begin again wearily. "You are mad, I tell you. A chair is a chair. That is its accepted meaning. It can have no other. I repeat, a chair is a chair."

"You know you are beginning to doubt it already. You have said it so many times that if I made one or two more passes with that word in front of the eyes of your ear, it would probably mean a dioptric or a grysbok" (thank you, Douglas) "to you, or perhaps a kite. Let it fly."

'The eyes of your ear — my God! — you're mad. A 'dioptric,' a 'grysbok,' a kite — *stop* or I shall go mad too.'

He was so greatly antagonized by this, to him, deliberate misuse of the Anglo-Saxon tongue that he maintained it was perfectly easy to do, that Gertrude was not serious about it but was just having a good time by mixing up a lot of words; that there was no technique or principle involved and that anyone could do it. And that, what is more, G. S. could be fooled by it and think it a serious attempt. "Try it!" I challenged. "Very well, I will. Give me a pencil and paper. I will do a portrait of Rubio and have it ready by tea-time." This was just after lunch one day. "Go ahead. I will come and get it at tea-time, and I will send it to Gertrude through a third person whom she'll never suspect, E. Grant Watson" (whose books are written in the good old-fashioned way, and very well too). "I will get him to say he doesn't endorse it, but that a friend of his has sent it to him to be forwarded to her for criticism, and will she graciously accord him an opinion as to the advisability of his pursuit of this method, his talent for it, etc. Agreed? ”

“ Yes, agreed.”

“ All right — tea-time, remember.” And I left him. I came back at tea-time and he pounced up at me from a corner of the sofa.

“ Go away,” he yelled in a murderous tone. “ I’m not done yet.”

“ Forgive me,” and I left the room.

At dinner-time I returned. He was walking up and down the room. “ Paul dear,” I said as gently as I could, “ come to dinner. It’s eight o’clock.”

“ I don’t hear you,” he said, no longer murderously but in a broken voice, “ I don’t hear you.”

I dined alone.

At bed-time I made one more attempt. He was sitting at the piano, head bent forward against the music-rack. This time I thought I had better be firm.

“ Paul, you must go to bed. It’s late. You have an early lesson to-morrow. Mühlen will be furious.”

He muttered from somewhere under his lowered head: “ Mühlen could be furious but Rubio not so, so not furious could Rubio be as Mühlen was as Mühlen is, because of the not chair — No, it was I who was furious about the chair — I can try that ‘ Mühlen furious but not about not furiously about a not chair.’ . . . Oh! My God.”

“ Paul dear,” I said, “ would you like me to play over one of those *Gesu gespracht* passages that I was so flippant about yesterday when one appeared for the eleventh time in the Bach B Minor Mass? I will play it nicely to-night, I really will, as many times as you like."

"Why did *Gesu* ever *gesprächt?*" he moaned.

I left him. I heard him come to bed very late. The next morning at breakfast I did not mention it, nor did he, but he left my room with a grim look in his eye and a batch of paper under his arm, a freshly sharpened pencil in his pocket. By lunch-time he reappeared and literally prancing with joy exclaimed: "I've done it. I've done it. It's very good. Here it is. Send it along." It really was very good — in Gertrude Stein's manner without being in any sense a parody. It was dispatched to Gertrude according to the plan already outlined. It came back to Grant Watson a week or so later with a note from her (which he kept, so I cannot reproduce it here) to the effect that if his friend had any literary gift at all, which she was in no position to judge from the one article submitted, it was most certainly temperamentally unsuited to the style he had so flatteringly chosen; he had best follow his natural writing direction, which was doubtless of a scholarly and conservative trend.

"Have a chair," I said to Draper, when he had finished reading the note.

"Yes, I will, thanks," he answered.

So I mixed him one.

. . . .

May Sinclair turned up at Edith Grove once or twice that season. A neat demure little figure in a Sunday-black-broadcloth suit bound with braid, a toque trimmed with

calmly folded wings of what looked like a very domestic
bird and a dotted lace veil holding it and her hair in
place. She never spoke a single word to me except
" Thank you " and " Good-bye," but you did not conceive of her as an uncommunicative person. The first
time she entered the studio I knew she liked it, though
she never said so. She walked carefully across the room
and choosing the biggest most luxurious floor cushion
of all, made of yellow and silver brocade in a design of
vine leaves (vine leaves, mind you, and she with folded
fowls' wings in her hair!), pulled it out with determination into the middle of the floor, and sat in the middle of
it, feet and legs tucked modestly under her black broad-
cloth skirt, veil still tightly tied about her head. There
she sat, through the night, listening and watching. At
one moment, after Alfred Cortot had finished playing
César Franck's *Prelude, Aria,* and *Finale,* on the piano,
she got up nimbly and taking off her coat, turned it inside
out, carefully folded it so that a cherry satin lining
gleamed in the light, and placed it reverently over the
back of a chair. Then she returned to her Bacchic cushion,
where she remained seated the rest of the evening. At
supper she lifted her veil just above her lips to sip a glass
of champagne, then pulled it down again.

Harry Melville, that ornament of London society and
very dear person, came often to the musical evenings.
He had a face of cream-brown sensitiveness, a thin aqui-
line nose, wide-opened black-brown eyes and the most
amazing hands. He talked incessantly and well. It was
his form of art and his medium of creation. He would

wait until a small audience collected and then begin. It was usually a narrative of some person or persons that he built up with exceeding care and a nice sense of composition. Witty, appreciative, a little malicious, he had a childlike desire for praise, and woe unto him who missed a finely spun point he would make in the course of his narrative. If he felt generously and tolerantly disposed toward you, he would give you one more chance, repeating it a little louder, fixing his wide-opened eyes on you to force the point, in case you missed it again, and punctuating every phrase with the amazing hands. They were beautifully shaped and constantly moving from delicately wrought wrists. If his conversation was the composition of a picture his hands were the colour of it. With a slightly lowered thumb, he could send dynasties toppling to the ground; with a slightly upraised one he could impertinently thumb his nose at a departing guest. With a sudden clench of them he could murder the lady who missed his point, and with a prayerful clasp he could worship at the shrine of the lady who did not. They were not the only shrines at which he worshipped. His first editions and inscribed copies were the delight of his life, and a fine painting filled him with pleasure. I spoke to him so much about his hands — indeed, he knew their value — that when he had them photographed by Man Ray he had one made for himself, one for Man Ray, one for a friend and one for me, or so he said. In any case it is a portrait of the man, those photographed hands, as no painted canvas could be.

He adored Sophie Tucker. What would I not give to

hear a conversation between them just once on the vaude-
ville stage! If only such things could happen. He complained bitterly about parties to which one was asked
where " a few, only a few, will be there," or where you
were begged to stay behind when all the great crowd left
and " a few, just a few of the ones that really count, will
stay." He said he hated them, they were always dreary
and contentious or dull. Give him the crowds, he said, the
bigger the better; and the hotter and stuffier it was and
the more difficult to get about, the better party he found
it. " Never let me remain amongst the dull flattered few.
Give me the amusing flattering many! "

.   .   .   .

There was a day in Florence when Mabel Dodge and
I had heard of a village for sale. We desired to buy it.
It was an old feudal estate, built around a court and com-
prising every period of architecture that had flourished
in Italy from the eleventh century to the late eighteenth,
when the family that owned it was forced to give it up.
Wings had been added to turrets, arcades had closed an
open side of the courtyard, as succeeding generations had
added what they needed or what pleased them. For
nearly a hundred years it had been occupied by peasants
as a village. It was large enough to house at least three
hundred men, women and children, had its own post
office, a few shops and possibly a prison or two in a
dungeon below ground. When we saw it, the villagers
were about to be turned out, and the place sold. We
wanted it, we wanted it terribly. Doubtless we felt that
in a place big enough for three hundred we could live

in amity with our constantly changing guests and still
see something of each other. In any case, we wanted it.
We began one of those scribbled computations on the
backs of envelopes and such, to discover whether we could
extract enough from our incomes to pay the first install-
ment or whatever that mysterious transaction is by which
people come into possession of houses. My computations
took a very short while; Mabel's much longer, but even
she decided in the end that it was beyond our reach.
Now she is building a hacienda all over New Mexico,
and the Sitwell family of England have bought the Italian village and retire to it in twos and threes, but never
fives. In other words, Osbert Sitwell and his brother
Sacheverell descend there with a retinue of servants and
cohorts of guests, but not until Sir George and Lady
Sitwell have left. Or Sacheverell and Edith and Osbert
will adjourn there a while, but leave it when wires arrive from London, announcing the imminent arrival of
Sir George. Now that Sacheverell is married and has a
son perhaps a different five will occupy it. The family
adores each other with such intensity that it turns occasionally into furious rows. Osbert commissioned Se-
verini, the gay and delightful Italian painter, to paint a
series of panels in the big dining-room, which he accomplished with true decorative style and in the real " fresco "
technique, a rare thing to-day. Sir George fell into a rage.
They were hideous! Distorted, ridiculous, not Georgian,
in fact! He wouldn't have it. He couldn't look at them.
He wouldn't look at them. " Very well, you needn't,"
conceded Osbert, " but don't destroy them. Let me have

some plain panels or covers of some sort made to conceal them from your injured sight." So a truce was called, and the tactful Osbert had fitted covers made to obliterate the panels during his father's occupancy; they are put on the minute Osbert leaves and taken off the minute Sir George leaves. Slip covers for Severinis, so to speak. Fantastic life. When Osbert — he is the only one that can do it — writes the history of his family to-day, it will be a real contribution to the annals of our time.

However, all this is a prelude to the fact that sometimes the Sitwells are in Florence and sometimes in London and, sometime in the future, will be all three in New York. When their residence in either of these places coincides with mine, I am happy, as they enchant me. Whether it was in Florence or London that Osbert and I first met, or somewhere in the air between, we can never either of us remember. Suffice it to say, we have met. In that year before the war he was moving pompously and resplendently about in a gallant uniform. He was sitting alone in the front row at Queen's Hall the night when Casals and Thibaud played the Brahms double concerto, but he would not come back to Edith Grove with us. Very alone, just then, he seemed. Writing poetry, living splendidly, entertaining perfectly, talking wickedly and well, he was a figure of pink and gold importance, walking in and out of concert halls, sitting in Drury Lane boxes and standing in great and small houses.

.   .   .   .

Lady Colefax, then Mrs. Arthur Colefax, came busily and attentively to some of the musical evenings. Her luncheons were already famous in London. She collected people from every corner of everywhere, with a flair for contrast as well as combinations, and you were apt to hear a stimulating controversy between Clive Bell and Sir Claude Phillips or Sczymanowski and Roger Fry before lunch was over.

Sczymanowski did, upon occasion, become controversial. When he and Arthur Rubinstein were first installed in 17 Edith Grove, part of which I had converted into amicably separate guest apartments, the first morning of their occupancy proved a momentous occasion in Edith Grove. I had sent the Irish angel to them with early tea, as her Gallic wit and sympathy could more readily cope with whatever instructions Karol might wish carried out in the way of bath, breakfast and other kindly offices. He did not speak English that year, and the Irish angel did not speak French. In spite of this, it seemed that Karol had managed to signal to her his desire for a hot bath. She had gone to the tub in his adjoining bathroom and lighted a gas-heater which was the only method of heating a bath on that side of the house. At the slight combustion of the gas into flame, Karol leapt from bed, and clutching a silken bed-jacket across his throat, began a terrified harangue in Polish, of which she understood not one word, but of which the terror was emphatically conveyed. He pointed to the gas-heater and at her and back to the gas-heater again. She, confused by his ominous gesture and by her inability to cope with it, flew from the room, rushed upstairs and through into my room, gasping out —

" Glory be to God, madame, the Polish gentleman has gone mad," crossing herself haſtily as she did so. Karol came running into the room after her.

" Karol darling, what is it? " I asked.

And then in French and Polish came the explanation. It was the dangers of a gas-heater that threatened him. It would blow up, the house would blow up. Everyone in it would be killed. Even unlighted they were a source of danger. The children should never be allowed to come near them. No match should be lighted in the same house with them. They were . . .

" But Karol, dear, we have used it for months. The old man who lived here before us used it for years. It's perfeĉtly safe."

" *Muriel, ma chère Muriel, je vous en prie* . . ." Seeing that he was in a real ſtate of apprehension which could not be calmed, I finally asked the Irish Angel to go back with him and turn the evil gas-heater off. She did not answer, and when I turned to see what had become of her, I found her cowering on her knees in a corner sending up some pleading prayer to God on high to proteĉt us all from this impending fate, which by now she was as fully convinced of as Karol himself. No chance of getting her to turn it off — nor would Karol allow anyone to do it but myself. He seemed to feel that I would be proteĉted by some magic which I could exert to quell the roaring ſtorm that by now was brewing below-ſtairs. The excitement had laſted at leaſt a quarter of an hour, and as the boiler heated in ten minutes, I began to be a little nervous myself. However, over I went, followed

by Karol still clutching his silken jacket, and the Irish
angel, muttering prayers, bringing up the rear with
bowed head. I crossed over into the bathroom of number
17 and turned out the gas-heater. From the doorway,
Karol sent up a Polish paean of relief, and from the hallway back of him, the Irish Angel sent up a Latin telegram
of thanks to the good Lord who had unquestionably saved
us in answer to her prayer.

" In any case, Karol, you can have a hot bath, and we
are all alive," I declared irritably.

" *Muriel, ma chère Muriel,*" Karol began once more,
with the sweat pouring down his face . . . and he proceeded to tell me in solemn and convinced accents that
he had known, he himself personally, he had known
seven persons — " *oui, Muriel, sept personnes* " — who
had been killed by gas-heaters. Literally seven, three of
whom had been intimate and deeply mourned friends,
two of whom had been relatives, less intimate and scarcely
mourned at all, but relatives, nevertheless, and two more
of whom had been servants, his personal servants. Yes,
seven people in his life had been killed by gas-heaters.
Seven. I looked into his eyes fixedly and said, " Karol,
now really, not seven. It is impossible."

" Yes, seven, Muriel. So it has happened in my life.
Seven deaths from gas-heaters." I said no more. Indeed,
what was there to be said? A man who had endured great
losses in such an unprecedented way, was set apart from
his kind and not to be judged accordingly. I looked at him
once more, firmly, searchingly, and he murmured again,
guiltily, a smile just beginning somewhere around his

eyes: " It is aftonishing, I know, but there it is — seven."
And I left him before the smile could reach his lips, and
that extraordinary sequence of disafters be relegated to
the limbo of unreality from which it sprang. I wonder
for whatever reason he evoked it thence that morning?
It was never mentioned again, and his hot bath was
accomplished in uninterrupted peace every day thereafter for weeks.

 .   .   .   .

He and Arthur spoke much of a friend from Poland
who was due to arrive. They built up a fantaftic and
unique figure for me in this friend. He was a Count with
vaft holdings in Poland. Forefts, valleys, fields and
ftreams made up his eftate. He was an expert agricultur-
ift, knew all about wheat and horses and fertilizers, and
at the same time was one of the moft sensitive beauty-
loving souls in exiftence. Quite capable was he of leaving
all his eftates behind him for months at a time, to possible
ruin and decay, in order to go and see a picture in Paris
he had read of, hear a conductor in Vienna he had been
told of, or examine a manuscript in the British Museum
whose exiftence there he had finally traced. Very erratic,
they said, a little hyfterical and at times morose and shy
to a degree that approached sullenness, but make no mistake about it, he was a connoisseur of the firft water,
nothing escaped him. He would love Edith Grove;
the tapeftries, the Ming ftatue, the screen, the music. But
terribly shy. They cautioned me not to frighten him;
to leave him alone, and let him take things in by himself.
By that time I was enthralled and begged them to bring

him at once — the very day of his arrival. Very good. The day came. They brought him.

I barely looked at him when he was presented. I was afraid of destroying this shy, sensitive, retiring, beauty-loving Polish landed proprietor. Fields of fertilizer and Flemish tapestry floated before my eyes. Ears of wheat springing from illuminated manuscript waved vaguely before me. Snatches of Chopin mazurkas interwoven with the cries of newly born calves filled my ears. What a man! Making myself as invisible, inaudible, and not there as physical laws permit, I waved him to an armchair in a secluded corner by the Ming statue, placed a small mother-of-pearl and lacquer table by his side, put a Canton enamel box of my best Russian cigarettes upon it, moved a huge porcelain vase of almond blossoms to form a fragrant screen between us, and glanced timidly through them at his face for the first time.

It was a suburban face. His cheeks were freshly coloured, as if a brisk walk from the station had sent the blood into them, after a short, pallid journey in a stuffy train. From behind gold-rimmed glasses, his eyes looked out with nervous alertness, as if strained from a too close scanning of the stock-market news. Blunted, well-kept hands fingered a vaguely Masonic watch-chain, and a gold tooth was perceptible under his upper lip as he lifted it in a reluctant smile. As these details registered themselves on my sight, the previous image I had created of him in my mind was necessarily shifted a bit to make room for this new visualization, but I persuaded myself that this was to his advantage. Only an extraordinary Pole could hide the higher ranges of mind and sensibility under such thick veils of commonplaceness: I became all the more eager to adventure through them and discover the rare treasures that lay behind. I muſt control my eagerness and wait until the shy defences fell; so I offered him a cup of tea. He leaped up from the armchair and, with an angry wave of ſtumpy arms, signalled his refusal, exclaiming in a petulant raucous voice and very Polish French, " Only seven hours have I been in this dismal country, and already twice I have been offered tea! In Poland, also, we drink tea. I do not want tea. Have you nothing else to drink or eat? I would like to eat. I am hungry — *hungry,* I say! " He barked the laſt ſtatement and, peering expeċtantly at me through the gold-rimmed glasses, sat down again.

I soothed him with affrighted apologies, and promised him whatever there was to eat or drink in the house, adding the information that in " this dismal country " one acquired the unfortunate habit of drinking a cup of tea and eating a slice of bread and butter of a late afternoon, and dining later. He vouchsafed no reply to this, but liſtened attentively to the inſtruċtions I gave to a servant, for whom I had haſtily rung. Hoping to divert him into patience by the sound of his own language, I essayed a few conventional phrases in that moſt difficult of all tongues, phrases that I had maſtered by the sweat of my brow and the kindness of dear Sczymanowski and the Kochanskis. Without looking up from the pleased contemplation of his nails, in which he had been occupied since the servant had left the room, he smiled sourly and said, in the same high petulance, " I beg of you, madame, spare me the desecration of my native language, which I, by the way, speak exceedingly well. Your French is bad enough, but acceptable. Your Polish is execrable." His nails still occupied him.

No help was forthcoming from Karol, who was immersed in discussion with Paul Kochanski and Rubinstein. The impossible combination of such consonants as " sczy," which present almost unsurmountable difficulties in the pronunciation of Polish, formed a hypnotizing sibilant soft rush of sound issuing from their lips. I retired into silence, quietly sipping my tea. After what seemed an interminable length of time, the servant returned with a tray of food, placed it on the table by my shy, sensitive friend's side, looked at him with furtive curiosity, and left the room. The proprietor of countless Polish acres did not look up or move. The glint of his highly polished nails as he moved them to and fro in the light was the only sign of life he made. I put down my cup of tea and said, " Would you care to eat now? "

" I wait," he answered. " When food comes, I eat."

" But," I exclaimed, " it is there beside you on a tray."

" That! " he exclaimed, pointing to the tray, " *that* is food? "

" Yes, it seems to be food," I muttered humbly. " At any rate, there is a platter of cold meat and some salad, some biscuits and cheese, and a bottle of cha —— "

" Salad! " he shouted. " But I do not eat any green food, and as for the cold meat —— " Here he seized upon the platter, brought it up close to his face, scrutinized it minutely through his gold-encircled glasses, and continued, " I thought it was the pattern of the china, it is cut so thin. However, I will eat it. If the champagne is not too cold, you may open it. Thank you."

I opened it, hoping the cork would fall into the midst of the Polish contingent across the room, and stop the ceaselessly flowing sound of their conversation, and bring them to some realization of my dilemma. It did not. It dropped humbly at my feet. The conversation in the far corner went on. My most recent guest had begun at once on the platter of too-thin meat, dispensing with such delays as knives, forks and plates might interpose. I poured him a glass of champagne, and after standing nervously about for a minute or two, left the room quietly, hoping not to distract his attention from the first pleasure I had been able to afford him, meagre as it was. It had been agreed that he should dine at Edith Grove that evening, and a carefully selected few were to make music for him during the night. The first hour of my acquaint-ance with him had been so defeating that I needed rest in which to gather up my scattered forces to renew the struggle. I was determined not to lose the rare value that would reward me, provided I won through to this unique personality. Could my Polish friends be mistaken? Was he, perhaps, not as sensitive and beauty-loving as they believed? No — this was heresy. They must be right. I would try again at dinner and, in the interval, trust to whatever beneficent effect food, tapestries, champagne and a fire, coupled with my absence, might have upon him. In the safe haven of my bedroom, I turned out the light and sank down exhausted on a sofa: there I remained until it was time to dress for dinner.

I came down into the small drawing-room promptly at eight, and found the inspired agriculturist sitting alone before the fire, scrutinizing the cover of a copy of *Punch*. He looked up pleasantly enough, and without rising said, "It would have been foolish to make such a long journey back to the hotel in order to dress, so I stayed here. The others preferred to dress. I hope they will not be too late. You have no clock? But I do not need to know the hour. I am hungry. It must be dinner-time. . . . Quite a nice frock you are wearing, though black is not your colour."

Happy to find him somewhat mollified, I assured him that dinner was ready, but that we would give our friends a margin of at least another ten minutes.

"Very well," he sighed, "though if your chef is really a good one, ten minutes is enough to spoil his dinner. However, it can't be helped," and he smiled almost graciously. A negatively amicable silence ensued. His eyes looked a little heavy, and fearing he would fall asleep, I ventured a tentative remark in a low voice:

"Karol tells me you are fond of tapestries. Do you like those two pieces?" pointing to two rather fine strips that hung either side of the small drawing-room fireplace. "They are Spanish."

"Spain is a country I do not care for. Neither do I care for Spaniards." This without raising his eyes.

Casals was to be one of the chief music-makers of the evening; Rubio was coming also, to offer the fine flower of his beautiful personality, as well as his cello playing. And my friend did not care for Spaniards! Life can be very difficult.

This particular difficulty was solved for the moment by the arrival of my other guests, and by concentrating on them and their needs I managed for the moment to crowd out my perplexities. We went in to dinner gaily enough. I put the precious Polish farmer at my right, and kept him constantly occupied with food and drink. The dinner happened to be sufficiently good not to arouse his criticism, and a special pail of champagne was put by his side. He did not speak, he did not sleep: he did eat. All was well.

Dinner safely over, we went down into the music-room for coffee. Ensconced in his armchair once again, he seemed almost at home. I felt some progress had been made.

Coffee was served. When it was offered him, he waved it away with the same angry gesture of the short arms he had used when faced with the tea-tray in the afternoon, and said, " Tea, please."

" I'm so sorry. You shall have some tea at once. I thought you disliked it."

" Only in the daytime I dislike it. At night, I drink much tea. Indeed, all through the night I drink tea. . . . In a glass, with lemon, please," he called out after the confused servant.

Tea, with lemon and a glass, was brought — much of it. I was going to master the problem of this man if it took a lifetime.

Other guests were arriving, amongst them the beloved Spaniards. I left to Karol and Arthur the ceremony of introducing them to the newcomer. It was time they did something about this situation. They appeared unconscious of its having become a situation. They had merely handed him over to me in perfect generosity, as a gift that should afford me the utmost pleasure, and in that entirely trusting Polish way had not concerned themselves further. Finding me absorbed and fascinated by him, they did not question the basis of either my absorption or fascination. They brought guest after guest to him with elaborate and vivacious explanations in Polish of who each person was and wherein his talents lay. They were received affably enough by the guest of honour, at that time on his third glass of tea.

More friends arrived. Violins and cellos were lifted out of cases, silken wrappings were removed, and music put in place on music-stands. This diverted me from my main interest of the evening. I breathed more easily.

The music began. It was Mozart's quartet in D Minor. Paul Kochanski, playing first violin, led it serenely through the limpid movement of its allegro moderato to the tender loveliness of the second movement. I glanced in the direction of the armchair, which had become as much the province of the propertied Pole as his country estate, and observed with relief that his eyes were closed in apparent ecstasy of listening, his hands at rest upon his knees. If he had sat thus on that imagined suburban train, one could have thought him asleep. But

172

here in Edith Grove, with the perfect purity of Mozart filling his ears, it must be ecstasy. Very good.

When the andante came to a close, and Kochanski and his fellow players (Casals was at the cello, Morales — still another Spaniard! — was playing second violin, Gertrude Bauer faithfully drawing the bow across her viola) danced into the clear gaiety of the minuetto, I glanced once again, feeling sure this was a pleasure to be listened to open-eyed. His head had sunk down on his chest, his hands had fallen from his knees, his mouth had dropped open, and Mozart or no Mozart, the sound of his breath through his open mouth was a clearer indication of sleep than ecstasy. I gave up. If he had the good sense to sleep when he wanted to, let him sleep. He did not awake, even as the sprightly variations of the last movement filled the room. He snored lightly on. A Beethoven trio for piano, violin and cello, followed the Mozart. It did not disturb him. I did not permit anyone to notice him. After the Beethoven, Arthur Rubinstein stayed at the piano and began to play a Chopin polonaise. Perhaps it was in a spurt of patriotism that the Count finally awoke. He listened attentively as Arthur tore brilliantly through it, and at the end turned smilingly, sleepily to me and said, " He plays well, my friend, does he not? "

" He does," I answered. I was beginning to know *this* man, and to put aside, finally and forever, the man who had been born of the description given me by his Polish friends.

It was time for supper and we adjourned to the dining-room upstairs. The table was laden with cold fowls, salads, small pink sweets for Chester, fruits, a chafing-dish for scrambling eggs, and a huge coffee urn. On a side-board was champagne; on a small table a pot full of tea, a glass, and a plate of sliced lemon. My friend (he was really becoming my friend, now that tapestries, music, the higher ranges of the mind, and the aroma of "beauty" were no longer troubling the air between us) beamed with pleasure, and ignoring the more solid foods on the dining-table, sat down beside the tea-table. I offered to bring him something to eat, but refreshed from his sleep, relieved at the clearer mutual understanding that was emerging, he refused very kindly and with a nice suburban wink, said he would wait until the crowd thinned out that had gathered around the big table, and then "eat a morsel of something."

There was in the house that night a lady who was caught in the tangled meshes of a violently jealous husband. He was a gifted and delightful man, but perhaps not quite sane. He felt that any thought or pleasure she experienced apart from himself was an act of disloyalty. This position he was ready to defend unto death — his death or anyone else's. He made any kind of relationship between them and friends almost impossible to maintain. Occasionally, as a relief from the tension of such a pathological emotion, he would drink with the same violence he exercised in jealousy. These periods were an admixture of peace and terror to her. It meant that he would absent himself for days at a time, which was comparative peace, but it also meant that he might return on the scene with a small pistol in one hand, the other murderously clenched. Doubtless this was more of a threat than a real danger, but one never knew . . . in any case it was not conducive to friendly intercourse. He suffered a few concerts with her, but she was seldom allowed to enjoy what music there was in the world for her to hear. On the rare occasions when his humour or absence permitted, she came to Edith Grove. Her pleasure was genuine, her taste impeccable, and her presence a delight. On this night, believing her husband safely sailed away on a sea of alcoholic oblivion, she had risked an hour or two with us. Thinking she would appreciate the strangely distributed values of my Polish landed proprietor, I brought her over to his tea-table. He looked at her carefully, and offered her some tea. I left them together.

The dining-room became less crowded. Some strayed back into the music-room, others sat in the small drawing-room: a few conservative ones left, and a scant dozen still hovered over the champagne.

A taxi-door slammed noisily in the street. The sound of frantic feet running across the sidewalk and up the front steps reached our ears, and loud rapping thuds on the door punctuated the steady ringing of the bell. The servants had gone to bed. One look from the so unfortunately victimized lady's eyes conveyed to me her fear that it might be her husband. I rushed to a window from which the front door could be seen. She was right: it was he. Pivoting unsteadily around the finger he held persistently on the bell, he was beating on the door with the butt of the small pistol he always carried and frequently flourished. I turned quickly to the few people in the room, and in some way managed to push them out of it. The lady herself flew upstairs. Messages were sent to the studio, begging the people there to be quiet, to get behind the screen, under the sofa — anywhere out of reach of this infuriated approach. The man might climb in a window if the door resisted him.

The party dispersed as if by magic, some rushing through the kitchen and basement into number 17, the house next door, which was connected in odd and sub-terranean ways. Finally everything was quiet — no sign of life — as the fracas at the door increased. Everything and everybody, that is, save my shy, sensitive, life-loving Polish guest of honour. Understanding little of the con-fusion but with unexpected willingness to acquiesce in the general movement, he had risen from the tea-table upon the flight of the lady, asking me nervously what was the matter.

I explained as quickly and succinctly as I could that there was a maniac at the door, with a desire to shoot someone, anyone. He was breaking down the door. He might get in at the window. He particularly wanted to shoot his wife — the lady with whom he had so recently shared his tea. Never mind why. The man was mad, but life was sweet. Wouldn't he please go somewhere out of sight? Yes, he would. It seemed too bad to be disturbed, but he would go, and with a look of patient resignation such as the plodding suburbanite might wear when re-quested by the conductor to step into the next car because

the one he was in did not go to his station, he started out
of the room, the last man in it. I assisted his progress by
gentle pushes from behind, and had almost steered him
by the big table when, alas! he saw a deep silver bowl
of *Pêches Melba* on it. With a leap of joy, he cried out
in the first really ecstatic tone of voice I had heard from
his lips, " Ah! *Pêches Melba!* I adore them. They are of
all things in life the most perfect. I must eat one."

" My dear friend, I beg, I implore you, don't stop
now for a *Pêche Melba.* I will send thousands every day
to your hotel. Stay here in my house forever, and I will
bring them to you! I will crate them to Poland, come
and grow them on your farm if you like, but you won't
live to eat them again if you stop to eat this one. The door
is breaking: we will both be killed. Go; for God's sake,
GO! "

My prayer fell on deaf ears. He sat down calmly in
front of the silver bowl and with tears of happiness
streaming from his eyes, bent low over it, and began
to eat a *Pêche Melba.* He finished it. Crooning voluptu-
ously in the elusively sensuous accents of his native
tongue, he smiled up at me from over the edge of the
bowl, and began on the next. He was evidently determined to eat them all.

The front door creaked ominously.

" If I must die, I must die. It is not important. He may
kill me, this maniac; he may kill you. To you, life is of
value: to me too, but not of more value than this *Pêche
Melba.* Truly, madame, you are a great woman, and my
friend. You understand the preparation of a *Pêche Melba.*

My compliments! I would like to go with you into safety, or even protect you and that irritating gentleman's wife, but I cannot — I *will* not — leave these peaches while there is yet one left to eat." He waved me on to safety with a gesture of grandeur and perfect understanding. I was conquered.

" You are a great man," I said. " I will stay here with you while you eat." I sat down opposite him. He made no sign of recognition. He was devouring a third peach.

The noise outside abated somewhat. The raging husband was wearing himself out. The door was still intact.

In the desolation of the deserted dining-room, over the ravaged remains of food on the table, I pushed a glass of champagne toward the " shy " Polish nobleman. I lifted my own glass and said, " Our values are different, but we would both die for them. Salutations."

I waited for him to take up his glass, but wiping away from his chin some drippings of raspberry sauce that had covered the peaches, and tears that had dropped from his eyes, he smiled, shook his head, and in a sudden blaze of complete friendship said, " No more champagne just now, thank you. I have come to the last peach. You will share it with me, yes? "

I nodded. He halved it carefully, slowly, found a plate, placed the morsel of peach reverently upon it, and handed it to me. I took it. There was a sound of faltering footsteps retreating down the steps, across the sidewalk, and into the night. In blissful silence we ate the last peach.

Then, over the champagne, we discussed the breeding of pigs in Poland and the Merrimac Valley.

178

The Polish Nobleman Who Faced Death for a Pêche Melba Stands in the Centre, But Was too Shy to Face the Camera. Even John McMullin, that Unique Californian, Screened Himself Behind My Black Lace Skirt, while Sozia Kochanska Exchanged Discreet Sczy's with Carol. Sczymanowski. Mrs. Edith Who Played Bravely as the Russian-Irish Mystic Sang, Is Protected by her Husband and Arthur Rubinstein, while Mrs. Bergheim Keeps Us and Her Lawn in Order

Mrs. Napier, who brought me to Henry James, took me to the house of her friends, Mr. and Mrs. Rowland E. Prothero. Mr. Prothero was one-time editor of the *Quarterly Review*. He had brought to it a sturdy scholarship and a clean, sandy sense of humour. His wife flitted about him in a soft small grey-dark flutter, through which her widely-opened round brown eyes made circles of kindly penetration. Her quickly moving hands brushed the dust of boredom out of the air that surrounded her, as the busy wings of small birds dislodge obstructing motes in sunlight. I see her mouth pursed in a little " o-o-o " of readiness for laughter, sympathy and surprise. They made the house they lived in, with its fine Adams ceilings and staircase, a place of cool well-bred delight where men and women they selected with careful variety met and went away refreshed. Gentle rotund Sir Ray Lankester, who issued suave scientific dicta *From an Easy Chair* in the London *Times,* was often there, telling you tales of whales and penguins that were amazing enough to be untrue. That desiccated echo of respectable scandal, John Cross, walked with a pale rattle through the rooms of the house, conveying a negation of all romance and seeming an impossible repository for even so remote and distinguished a passion as George Eliot's; and yet this very echo within him was the only voice of life that kept him from the grave. You felt that Mr. and Mrs. Prothero nicely valued him thus, kindly offered him as such, with no hint of malice or side-smiling. How else could they have placed us side by side at dinner?

Robin de la Condamine, who had been party to our Florence fortnight, threaded through my life. Formulation of shattering innuendoes, writing one book and acting brilliantly when it pleases him, are not his only gifts. He has the gift of friendship. During the two Italian years of my life, as well as the later English period, no problem however slight could be concealed from his heart's discernment, nor could it be too complicated for the skilful untangling his quick, elaborate mind could effect. In the cool, dark, high rooms of his apartments in Florence, difficulties that had assumed inflated proportions outside were reduced to governable size. In the fantastic columned drawing-room of his London house, whose rare sunlight slid over silver tables and through small trees of crystal, jade and amber, ponderous melancholies dispersed.

His appearance was of a puzzled contradictoriness. His fair hair at times seemed the last statement of youth at the top of his body: at others, it looked like the first thin, dun capitulation to age. His eyes could be translucent cups of candour that changed under your very gaze into deceptively rusty little knives to wound with. His nose cried out in impertinence, though it could retreat into decorous oblivion upon occasion. The end of a smile that appeared on his lips was not predictable: it might drivel into blank idiocy or too legible a sneer. The expression of his body was not less volatile. His hands rhymed with the rest. This native trick of contortion was doubtless the impulse at the root of his sporadic acting, which he brought under control and developed into a technique of subtlety and power. Mistrustful of his own resistance to such facile gifts, he created a deterrent in the form of a stutter and a club foot.

I use the word " created " advisedly, if it can be used at all, because I knew him before he stuttered either in his speech or foot. He often discussed the desirability of acquiring just these checks against the dangers of over-sensitized physical response, and gradually accomplished it. Needless to say, the phenomenon represented for him something of greater significance than acting, but I am recording it in the light of his public demonstration, rather than his private avowals. In pursuit of his aim, he had formed the habit of following cripples in the street, and on the rare and blessed occasions when he met with man or woman who was endowed with the special object of his desire — a club foot — he would leave me stranded on a street-corner, at the door of a church, on the banks of a river, anywhere, while he rushed prayerfully after and past his victim. Or was *he* the victim?

In any case, after years of application he has now one leg much shorter than the other, a vaguely misshapen foot attached to it, and, crowning glory! the huge, thick, solid boot he so long envied.

The process of evolving the stutter was less simple to observe. In the smooth flow of his speech, he would throw a stone of silence or a swift mirthless stick of laughter: he would bark at the echo of his voice like a dog barking at his shadow: he could hold up his beautifully modelled phrases and break them into a dance of graceless, uncontrolled movements, like an ill-guided marionette. Finally, he juſt naturally ſtuttered. Pathologiſts could explain it otherwise, but he has no need of them. Once on the ſtage, his voice and feet move in perfeſt freedom and obey without impediment whatever command he lays upon them. His performance of Herod in Oscar Wilde's " Salome " was the fineſt I have seen. At Edith Grove, he sang verse after verse of gruesome old Scotch and English ballads, accompanying himself at the piano, and never once entering the province of music.

He maintained that if you were not possessed of a for-tune, you muſt have a firſt-rate cook or a firſt-rate scandal in your life, to be a success in the society of the world. Happily he was rich, and however good or bad his cook was, his food was marvellous. . . . He managed to wear about himself a darkly glimmering implication of murders and thefts in the paſt or immediate future, although his gaiety and wit were ever present. He may not sound like a haven of peace in troubled times, but he was. No grotesque enaſtment of his life is so solid as his aſt of friendship. He is ageless and belongs to no time-space in my life more than another, so I put him juſt here, until I do or do not see him again.

. . . .

It is ſtrange to realize how small a place the theatre occupied in my London years. De la Condamine's *Herod* ſtands out as one of the few memorable performances. Sir Herbert Tree dallied with Shakespeare. Arnold Ben-nett's play, *Mileſtones,* recalls a pleasant piſture of a diſtinguished lady spreading out her full taffeta skirts

over a tuffet as she sat down on it, saying in hopefully
pregnant voice, " The future . . ."

A play called *Hindle Wakes,* by Stanley Houghton,
seemed radical and disturbingly just, though to-day it
might be merely dull. *Fannie's First Play* was diverting. There were the musical comedies. In Lehar's engaging *Gipsy Love* Gertie Millar and Sari Petrass were
very differently fascinating, and Berry was funny as
only an English comedian can be. I seem to remember
taking a box for the run of the play in order to hear his
great line in the last act when I needed to. After a scene
where, thanks to everyone's efforts but his own, a castle
and its inhabitants are freed of the baleful influence cast
over them by the gipsy lover, he made a prancing, timorous inspection of the deserted castle hall, found it safely
empty, and with an inimitably witty assumption of courageous efficiency, shrugged his shoulders, waved a care-
less hand and said, " In the words of the great French
poet — *voilà!* " It was a singularly comforting slogan of
ineffectiveness that never lost its value for me.

Ethel Levey arrived from America and swaggered
rhythmically across the stage in that stylish stride of hers
to greet thrilled London audiences with a *Hullo! Miss
Ragtime*. It was in this very good revue that I heard
Irving Berlin's classic *Alexander's Ragtime Band* for the
first time. I shall never be satisfied until I hear it developed as a fugue for orchestra. There is more musical
meat in a few of Irving Berlin's phrases than . . . I will
restrain myself. The music of Irving Berlin is not a subject that belongs to London before the war. It is due to

the strain of listening during subsequent years to many less felicitous attempts to attain a new time-shape in music, that he emerges in single importance for me.

There were, thank God, the English music-halls! Here one could see George Robey, clothed in the sad, soggy raiment of an English lodging-house keeper, tawdry earrings hanging in doubtful embellishment from his tired ears, as he would lean exhaustedly on a broom-stick and wail, " I 'ave ter SWEEP the floors, MYKE the beds, EMPTY . . . 'eaded fool that I am," into the audience's delightedly apprehensive ears. Here one could feel the deft pathos and sagacious gaiety of the English cockney in the swift pattering songs and extravagantly buttoned coats of Albert Chevalier. Marie Lloyd's comprehensive wink at the right moment could reduce the most earnestly inflated virtue to ludicrous pretence, but her smile was a pledge to the world that the virtue of humour remained intact. The kilt of Harry Lauder flared in pleated promises of gallantry, wavered in sworls of drunken exuberance, or clung meagrely about his funny niggardly knees as he sang and hiccoughed and laughed his Scotch heart out in raucous sonority. Once, on the day in 1912 when the news of the wrecked *Titanic* reached London, he stopped in the middle of his laughter and hiccoughs, walked straight to the footlights and, shocked into artless simplicity, sang *Rocked in the Cradle of the Deep*. Never again can Harry Lauder sing a song so badly or so beautifully: no other audience of his will ever hear him thus.

Fred Emney in *A Sister to Assist 'Er* was a joy to

me. When he appeared in a garret doorway, staggeringly disguised as a rich sister of high estate, in the most amazing conglomeration of feathered and ruffled shabby splendour that any one old woman ever accumulated, to rescue an aged feeble gin-soaked crone from a distressful situation concerned with arrears of rent, there was always a breathless moment of silence before the house broke into uproarious mirth which the subsequent developments evoked. As the disguise broke down under the suspicious perseverence of the impatient landlady, helped by plentiful nips from a bottle of gin, and the three old hags fell into a frenzy of drunken poverty-stricken abuse, Emney rose to heights of farce that were not far removed from tragedy. The enthusiasm into which John McMullin and I were plunged upon first witnessing this scene, however, remains pure farce. It happened this way. One day in the late spring of our first London year, Paul Draper and I had wanted to take a look about the English countryside, so we took a motor and John, — still liking him very much indeed (I never wanted to look at a hat without him, to say nothing of the countryside), and started off. I seem always to be making that poor, dear man start off somewhere. At some provincial town on the road, we spent the night, and after one of those depressing dinners of pale beef, paler greens, and potatoes of death-like pallor, John and I fared forth to see what the town had to offer in the way of amusement. In the main street we found the one and only music-hall, bought tickets and went in. Billed as one of the chief attractions of the evening was Fred Emney in *A Sister to Assist*

'Er. The name was unknown to us. We anticipated none of the rare amusement that was vouchsafed us. To us, he was a discovery; he was a genius. He must be brought to London at once with his company, and I would arrange a party for him. London must not be deprived of this performance. Names of managers and cast were feverishly inscribed. What a treasure to find in the provinces! We brought excited reports to Paul. We must rush back the next day and arrange it. We did rush back. We even began to " arrange it." We didn't get far. Kind friends strait-jacketed us first, and then proceeded to inform us that Fred Emney and his act had been off and on the London music-hall stage for the greater part of twenty years, that children and grandparents knew the act by heart, that an occasional year's tour in the provinces was by way of being a welcome respite for even the most loyal of London audiences (and they are the most loyal in the world), that we would be quietly put out of the way if we attempted to go any further with our arrangements, and that, in short, we were a couple of demented loons from the American provinces ourselves, and had best leave the introduction of music-hall genius into London to the Londoners. Ah, well; it would have been a grand party, if they had left us alone. . . .

There was a rickety little red-headed straw man whose name will not come back to me, but whose high-pitched quavering voice rumbles about in my ears as I see him stumbling vaguely across the stage, head nodding fitfully, holding a tiny tin can by its handle, and singing in de-

voted futility, " Foooaoaoa — rrr — r I'm-m-m-m- takin'
m' feaeather his teaeaea."

Robert Hale could contribute something of value to the
debates on companionate marriage if he would give to
American audiences his one-sided dialogue with a suddenly recognized, long-loſt friend, whom he pretends
to discover in the theatre. He greets him with surprised
pleasure, and proceeds to queſtion him as to the chief
events and general welfare of family friends. Diseases of
the old, dissatisfaćtions of the middle-aged, rebellions
of the young are revealed in the queſtioning. And then
he asks tenderly for news of Mabel; " Mabel — yes,
Mabel . . . you know — Mabel. . . . How is she? "
There is a pause while the invisible, inaudible friend
relućtantly gives him the lateſt news of Mabel.
Robert Hale ſtraightens up, visibly affećted, and
cries out in accents of outraged incredulity: " What!
AGAIN?!? "

Yes, thank God, there were the London music-halls.
Between them and the Russian Ballet, whatever need I
had for the particular illumination of life the theatre
gives was filled.

. . . .

Diaghilev gave to London that season a dramatic dancing fare varied enough to satisfy the moſt jaded appetite.
Romantic ladies in traditional ballet skirts of white tulle
summoned a languishing pale-haired youth in a black
velvet jacket from a deep wood with amorous waves of
reed-like arms, to the deftly-woven music of Chopin in
Les Sylphides. A bird with wings of flame flew to the

enchanted release of an imprisoned court of dwarfs and potentates in Stravinsky's *L'Oiseau de Feu*. Savagely triumphant figures of marauding men and women emerged from sombre brown tents to celebrate their victory with rhythmic thrashing of bows and arrows on earth through orange-burning air that was invaded by the themes of Borodin in *Prince Igor*. Schumann's *Carnival* was a background against which delightedly frightened maidens in taffetas and muffs, defended themselves against the frolicsome advances of pirouetting youths in long-tailed cloth coats and short high hats. Eunuchs, who — in the absence of their battling but exacting Caliphs — failed in their duty, were felled to the floor of splendid palaces by the returning warriors, as the lustful golden women of their charge swooned in pursuit of one boy who gleamed dark through faint chiffon trousers: this was the picture of Rimsky-Korsakov's *Scheherazade*. A being who was the impassioned questioning of life asking the reason of its birth, capered its way through groups of gaping holiday-makers at country fairs into hurtful love with the lovely puppet of femininity who beguiled them, and in the tragic isolation which all such questioning begets, died with hands of clear grief outstretched for new living. Only the music of Stravinsky could shape such a need and give it the permanence of *Petrouchka*. A delicately monstrous creature looked askance at life and death, rippled through and beyond the curious archaic desires of a Greek girl, carrying with him on to the safety of a bleak rock a dangerously soft fragment of her clothing into which he sunk his loneliness. Thus, according to Debussy, did a faun occupy one sunlit afternoon. In *Sacre du Printemps,* Stravinsky conveyed the trembling blood-fear of groups of human beings as they witnessed the darkening of suns, and made the wasted offering of a virgin life to palliate the hunger of cosmic appetites: moons and suns as well as earth must feed or dance in hunger. In a warm, dark centre of red rose, a sleepily dancing débutante of the '50's brought into her fresh bedroom romance from a ballroom: through her wishful dreams, the figure of her cavalier danced in elegant acquiescence, to disappear through the window into rose-red illumined space as she awoke, — all to the sugaring measures of Weber's *L'Invitation à la Valse* in *Spectre de la Rose.*

Diaghilev brought this about. He invented, combined, arranged and directed the movements of human beings and the music that would best support them. From those who could create it, he exacted the best, or selected it from what was already there. He gave to Nijinsky the great rôles, allowing him the freedom of interpretation that genius does not abuse.

Of all dancers I have seen, Nijinsky alone could use his body as a symbol of imponderable ideas while it moved in fluid physical intensity. The world of canvas scenery, costumed bodies, and painted faces, was his reality. It was Nijinsky himself who leapt out into space in red rose-petalled grace in *Spectre de la Rose:* it was an uninhabited hulk of heavily breathing man that rose from the thick mattress held outside the window by six pairs of strong hands, to cushion his fall. The thin green-white mask of paint under long pale hair was the real face of Nijinsky, as he ran between pasteboard trees and flitting tulle skirts in *Les Sylphides:* the coarse-grained flesh of his sweating features beneath was an illusion of the man. He stepped into the shining dark lust of his own muscles when he blacked himself for the seduction of an Oriental court in *Scheherazade*. Atop the flimsy impermanence of a tottering show-booth in a country fair, the soul of Nijinsky questioned God with little useless folded hands, while unanswering crowds of spectators revolved in dead merriment below. . . .

After such performances, in Edith Grove he ate and drank with incurious stolidity, moved unnoticeably from room to room, smiled without meaning, and spoke rarely. So he nourished and maintained the living automaton that belonged to him, in order to use it for living during the segment of eternity vouchsafed him on the stage. There he remains forever alive, while his alien, useless body now functions in irksome waiting for its death.

Karsavina held her lovely woman's body in perfect readiness for whatever dancing meaning music deposited therein. She is, or was under Diaghilev's hypnotizing direction, the most truly musical dancer of her sex. No heavy curve of passion or light high line of gaiety in music found her unprepared. She danced on her toes or the soles of her melancholy feet; she danced on wings, she danced with the tips of her fingers and the back of her bowed neck. She was the right balance of human gesture for Nijinsky's moving code of abstractions.

190

Nijinsky's sister was touched by the same genius that invaded him. She swayed in sad lunatic rhythms, stood still in measured echoes of death, and in *Sacre,* convulsed her body in sacrificial frenzy.

Léon Bakst and Nicholas Roerich designed costumes and scenery of brilliant boldness or rich subtlety for these savage dramas and sophisticated comedies that were presented nightly in Drury Lane Theatre, and made of it a building of romance and delight in the year 1914.

Ballets alternated with operas, in which Chaliapin reigned supreme. The splendour of his Boris never dimmed. In the first act, as he walked out of the cathedral in which he had been crowned, his very step conveyed triumphant majesty of state, before the bells which acclaimed him rang out from towers and echoed in the roof of his mouth.

Pierre Monteux conducted as a rule, though Sir Thomas Beecham was responsible for some of the less memorable performances. Monteux often returned with us to Edith Grove, his viola tucked under his untiring arm, eager to participate in whatever music was forthcoming on the evening's program. It became almost impossible for me to enjoy any house but my own. I often looked forward with lively pleasure to parties in other houses, gracious invitations to which I had delightedly accepted: and yet, on the given day — or more often, night — I would find myself unaccountably speeding homeward from Drury Lane or Queen's Hall, the motor filled with friends, cellos and flutes, stopping on the way for food if the larders of Edith Grove were unprepared. Taxis, telephones and telegraphed regrets did the rest, and the midnight air of Edith Grove would be filled once more with lovely shapes of sound.

. . . .

Among other diversions of the London years, horse-racing was not neglected. In England it has an established dignity which the stock market of America has not yet achieved. Betting can be transacted by telephone with a fair amount of excitement. To feel a thousand pounds slide out of your life over a slender wire is a sensation that reaches you bathed in certain dream-like thrills, as you drink black coffee from a small gold cup at home. It is well to have the coffee strong. To see a Chinese statue riding into your life on the sweat-shining neck of a gleaming brown horse, as it reaches just far enough beyond other nervous necks to win, is a solid pleasure that makes the turf spring light beneath your feet.

Paul Draper found it an absorbing pastime, and — while it lasted — an astoundingly successful one. He became a scholar of racing form, with cipherings and computations that were mysterious hieroglyphics to my unenlightened mind. There was, to be sure, a horse called *Jerry M.* who ran in the Grand National one year, and whose antics in the paddock were so endearing that I placed a feverish five pounds on him. He won.

The part that horse-racing has played in my life deserves a book to itself, equally with Henry James and Norman Douglas. Suffice it to say here that it played a part, and that I am grateful to it for proving to me that losing is as valuable as winning . . . always provided the coffee is strong.

Tea will do. There came a day at the end of the 1914 racing season when Paul went to the Derby, and I did not. Proof of the advantages of losing had not been lacking during the preceding months, though it had not altered the fundamentals of life at Edith Grove. When he came back from that particular Derby, it was at tea-time. Sozia Kochanska was with me when Paul came in with Arthur Rubinstein and a quiet, humorous little cleric from that temple of distinguished failure, Groton School. Paul was greyly pale. Arthur was strangely flushed: the little cleric less quiet than usual. All three emanated a disturbed alarm. Two drank their tea very quickly. Draper drank none at all. Dear Sozia's protecting friendliness sensed an imminent gloom descending, and so she took the clerical gentleman and Rubinstein up the stairs from 19A to the small drawing-room of number 19 Edith Grove. Paul and I were alone.

He grew greyer and then said:

" All the money is gone. It has been going for a long while. The last went this afternoon — *all* of it."

" Will you have a cup of tea? " I asked.

" Muriel, you don't understand me. I tell you, all the money is GONE. You have not got any more. I have not got any more. There *isn't* any more. It is all gone," he reiterated.

" I do understand," I replied, " but I tell you the tea is *not* all gone. There is plenty more. Will you have a cup? "

"You are mad," he said . . . but he did not want a cup of tea.

.   .   .   .

He did want more music. I wanted more music. The blessed and faithful friends wanted to make it. So the air in Edith Grove was not stilled. There was the house. It was June of a most splendid London season. The miracle maids and the Irish angel would not leave us: they were agreed upon this. The chauffeur believed that no one should go to the opera on foot, nor yet in taxis, and there were those comforting magic bits of pink, blue and yellow pasteboard in a reassuring little packet on my desk, that meant many more nights of Drury Lane delights to come — so we did not let the motors go at once. The diminutive footman, who broke more vases than all the other servants I have had before or since (he had a passion for dusting them), was reluctantly incorporated into the staff of the small cherished hotel of our first descent, where he led a less uncertain but, so he subsequently assured me, " not 'arf as sprightly " a life.

Sprightly the life at Edith Grove may have seemed to him, but he used to present a figure of stunned solidity, of which only the eyes moved, as he stood erect at the door of the motor as I passed by him in outrageous trappings. His gaze would be fixed on some brilliant dangling jewelled harness which I had elected to fasten on my head (doubtless inspired thereto by the Florentine horses of Carl Van Vechten's embittered comparison), and he would remain in a trance, his hand on the door handle, but not shutting the door, until I would cry out: " There is no more of me to-night, Burton. Shut the door." He was not an indispensable member of the household, as can be imagined.

The butcher, baker and candleſtick maker, to say nothing of the floriſt, woodman and dressmaker, behaved with the courtesy and patience which they so perfeЄtly command. They suggeſted that another year or two would bring financial readjuſtment. I suggeſted that they might be over-confident. They politely countered with a generous expansion of the two years into ten, and offered to re-ſtock wherever there was need. With difficulty I resiſted — perhaps not always. It is more than ten years now and small compensation have they received for their pains, yet not one of them — and we have had voluminous correspondence — has ever withdrawn the patient courtesy they then proffered.

With such inducements to continue for the balance of a season a life that could never repeat itself, I determined to enjoy it. The end would come soon enough, and what would that be but a new beginning?

The cellar, thank God and Paul Draper, was well filled. The music, again God and Paul be thanked, was without end. Friends do not fail. This is not a fitting place for thanking them, but I despair of fashioning a fairer one, and will not let them go unthanked.

And life at Edith Grove progressed in enchanted ſtaves, where notes of disaſter found no sounding place. Money was not. The passivity of its absence did not diminish the aЄtivity of life's present values. It is conceivable that disasters of real import were displacing the air about them in such a way as to render invalid all lesser experiences, crowding them into the minor significance they later inevitably assumed.

A man in Sarajevo, — where was Sarajevo? — killed an Austrian Archduke . . . shot him and his Duchess as they sat in the archducal motor-car on the way to the Town Hall of Sarajevo. Why? Doubtless the fanatical act of a nervous young patriot or the futile plot of ego-starved peoples. Another of those remote Near East problems! For a day it filled the papers to the exclusion of the Irish question. Editorials of polite sympathy for the Austrian emperor, to whose manifold sorrows one more had been added, renewed memories of the ill fate that pursued the House of Hapsburg; a week of Court mourning was announced; mildly interested conjectures as to the effect on the isolated political situation were formulated, and the papers were again free to dedicate their columns to the troublous situation in Ireland, women's rights, complaints of Maurice Ravel anent the Drury Lane performance of his ballet, and the honours accorded the visiting British fleet by the German Emperor and the Czar and Czaritza of Russia.

June melted into July. In the window-boxes magenta and white stocks filled the rooms of Edith Grove with the spiced magnificence of fragrance they breathe. White awnings at the windows kept out the noon-day sun: open fires forestalled the midnight cool. In spite of music-filled nights, breakfasts were early, because the two sons were so pleasant in the morning. Sisters and brothers of

Paul's and mine were arriving and departing, some with pleasant sons and daughters of their own, all in varying degrees of trepidation concerning our future, about which we were excitedly unoccupied. I knew life could not ſtop for me: I had not had enough of it. How it would be lived was a matter of changing detail. The essential values were an imperishable challenge which would not be denied. In the meanwhile, it was July in London . . . 1914, an era of my life that muſt be lived out to its laſt moment. I knew with increasing conviction that it would not happen again.

My earrings grew a little longer, head feathers a little higher, the champagne a shade colder in the July heat; flowers were plentiful, and friends more dear. Sackcloth and ashes would have been more seemly, could I have truly worn them. But, alas! oh, happy fate! at a tender age, I had accompanied my God-loving father to a bank in the Merrimac Valley and ſtood on tiptoe beside him as he pushed a check for one hundred dollars under the golden bars that separated the princely cashier from the common herd, and liſtened to his requeſt for ten ten-dollar bills. We were going to Boſton. Never before or since has it seemed so desirable and glittering a place as in that moment, while I waited for the fortune we were to spend in it. We waited — not long. The cashier returned, and in the clarion tones those lordly creatures adopt, said, "Sorry, Mr. Sanders; your account won't carry that." And he pushed the magic-coloured bit of paper back into the drab world.

My father looked at it a minute, smiled down at me,

and tore it up. Then he pulled his checkbook out of one of a thousand pockets, wrote out a check for ten dollars, and slid it under the golden gateway once more, saying, " Well, give me ten ones."

The perplexed minion of riches went away, and after what seemed to me a lifetime of suspense, returned with ten one-dollar bills, pushed them out to my father, and looked out gloomily between his bars. . . . We went to Boston.

Blessed be my father whose whole life was the most valuable lesson a child could receive. If Boston could be conquered by ten ones, surely a London season need not be lost. After all, I had ten ones, and there was still plenty of tea. Even Paul was drinking it again.

. . . .

He was in the very act of drinking a cup of tea, one July afternoon, when he decided to go to Germany and give to its people the beauty that Mühlen had helped him receive from the songs of their country. The London season was nearing its close. Only a few more weeks of ballet, one more performance of *Rosenkavalier* at Covent Garden, perhaps one new feathered turban on my head and jewels in my nostrils instead of in my ears, possibly a first tooth appearing in the mouth of our youngest son, and a second one leaving the mouth of our eldest, more and more music in Edith Grove (but it could never end), and we would be off to Steyning once more. There would be one one left for a cottage at 2 *s.* 6 *d.* a week. I would do something: I did not know what. " In the words of the great French poet — *voilà!* " The more we discussed it,

the wiser it seemed. At what better moment could he arrive in Germany, and catch the song-listening populace
before it scattered into summer listlessness? Mühlen
wished it. It might bring money into usable activity again.
In our lazy hurry we did not stop to realize that lieder-
singing is a gift from which many benefits accrue, but seldom one of commercial gain. In any case, Paul left.

There was a farewell party for him. All the closest
friends were there. We were gay but restless. Thibaud
was cutting off locks of his hair and throwing them out
the dining-room window and into the aromatically sleeping stocks. He would not play that night, but was very
entertaining. He told me Ysaye was coming to London
soon, and wanted to come to Edith Grove. He proceeded
to give an account of a wicked molestation of Ysaye's
exhausted sleep, of which, once upon a time, he had been
guilty.

It happened that together they were crossing the Channel from France to England, on a very tempestuous day.
Ysaye, a painfully bad sailor, was terrified and very sick.
Thibaud comforted and tended him with every solicitous
care of which his generous nature is capable. It was no
easy task, as Ysaye had an important concert engagement
for that evening, and felt with every wave that he would
not only be unable to fulfil it, but would never again in
this life draw a bow across a selected bit of catgut. It was
very pertinently unthinkable.

Thibaud distracted him, prayed over him, fed and un-
fed him, and finally brought him safely to port. Weak
from fatigue, Ysaye huddled in a corner of the train until

it reached London, and there, almost crying from the exertion of his sufferings, begged Thibaud not to desert him, to companion his despair and stay with him at his hotel until such time as he would have to make an appearance on the concert stage.

Thibaud, still kind, consented. They made off for the hotel, and once in the lobby, Ysaye with a weak wave of the hand and a green countenance, cast off all the tedious details of registering, luggage, choice of rooms, telephones to managers, letting them fall on the less enfeebled shoulders of his friend. He must sleep. That was all he asked of life — sleep. He must have it. He could no longer stay awake. Undisturbed sleep, not to be interrupted save by the last call for the concert hall. Please, would Thibaud see to it? Where was the key? SLEEP! and he tottered bulkily off into an elevator and away, key in hand, a wan smile of childlike trust moving timidly about his sickened lips.

Thibaud, still kind, but a little disinclined to dedicate the rest of his life to such friendly offices, nevertheless carried out the duties imposed on him, sent up the luggage, gave strict instructions that no one under any circumstances whatever should be allowed to communicate in any way with Monsieur Ysaye, telephoned managers, and at last retired rather wearily to his room, there to remain until the given moment in which he was to summon the great virtuoso to his labours of the evening. A friend indeed.

In the quiet of his room he began to review the day. It had been a tiresome one. Ysaye, after all, need not have been reduced to such utter wreckage by an ordinary attack of seasickness. Anyone might be seasick! It was not death-dealing. Once on land, he should have recovered. Could one be seasick on land? Certainly not. It began to irritate him. He did not like the hotel of Ysaye's choice. Why the devil had he come there? Utter nonsense to stay cooped up in one of its rooms for another two hours, nursing the slumbers of his friend. After all, he was a fiddler himself. He had an engagement to fulfil the next day. The limits of friendship had been transgressed. With mercurial quickness he became angry. He'd be damned if he'd stay there another moment. He telephoned down to the desk to ask the number of Ysaye's room, and then flung himself out of his own and down the corridor. The burden of waking Ysaye could be left with the desk. He would not do it — not he.

And then, as he passed an innocent-looking doorway in an isolated wall of the hotel corridor, his eye inadvertently perceived two neat little capital letters, international symbols of necessitous relief offered to ladies and gentlemen who travel the world, printed in decent blue legibility on a small white sign affixed to the door. His course became dazzlingly clear to him. He would spare the hotel staff the duty of waking Ysaye: the guests, in this case the "lady-guests," must share it between them. He wrenched the sign from its place, pocketed it, and rushed happily down the corridor to the door of Ysaye's room. Upon it, with silent, inspired skill, he fastened the guiltless little sign, and left it to do its involuntarily wicked work. . . .

An elevator took him down; he went to the desk, asked for his bill, and sent up for his luggage. The polite proprietors, surprised at this sudden departure, asked if he were dissatisfied in any way.

"Dissatisfied?" exclaimed Thibaud, *"Mon Dieu, non!* In my life, I have never been more perfectly satisfied. I am leaving. *C'est tout."*

And he left.

Yes, Ysaye forgave him. They adored each other, in fact, and Thibaud would bring him to Edith Grove the minute he arrived. But he would not play that night. I tried to tempt him with Chausson's lovely work for violin, piano and cello, a work of which he was very fond; but he insisted that I did not really like the French school of music, and was merely being polite, so I left him alone, throwing his hair into the flowers. It was obvious that he did not *want* to play. Arthur Rubinstein attacked him next. No, it was too hot to play, he mumbled over his shoulder. Arthur became annoyingly persistent.

"Very well," Jacques flung his body quickly around to face Arthur as he spoke. "Very well; I will play the Brahms viola concerto if you will play it with me."

Rather a staggering order. The violin score was not in our library, nor was the piano transcription of the orchestral score there either. Violinists do not consider it as part of their chamber music repertory! Arthur accepted the challenge. I was amazed. "But, Arthur," I protested, "I don't believe you have ever seen a piano score, much less played it."

" Why should I have seen it? I am not a violinist. I am not a conductor. But I know the work very well. I have heard it. Come, Thibaud; we will begin." He walked powerfully out of the dining-room, through the small drawing-room, and down the stairs into 19A.

Thibaud, suddenly alive, followed him, flinging what remained of his black hair back from his forehead. From different corners of the house, vaguely disorganized guests gathered under the studio roof. Even Chester left his pink food. " The Brahms violin *concerto!* You're crazy. These two Americans have driven you *all* mad. What are you going to play it from? " he asked them.

" Memory," they answered, at the same moment.

" Don't be foolish. It can't be done," he fumed, but remained bolt upright in the biggest chair he could find to sit in, as they walked over to the piano, a little slowly, to be sure.

The Irish angel flew into the room. " Madame," she wailed, " it's long past Smudge's " (a nickname that will never leave my youngest son) " feeding time. He's crying with hunger."

" Give him a bottle," I commanded, between my teeth.

" But, madame — of what? You know he's never had anything but — "

" Of milk, of anything — I don't know. Wean him. Leave me alone. I can't come upstairs now. Wean him. Don't you know how to wean a baby? It's perfectly simple. Just give him a bottle," and I turned away from the problem with heartless determination, her faithful

" Glory be to God, madame. You're *terrible,*" sounding in my ears. . . . She managed it somehow.

Douglas came up to me, and said, " You're getting a little hysterical, Mew. What's the matter? Have you been — "

" None of that now, Doug. I'm all right. Leave me alone. Thibaud and Arthur are going to play the Brahms violin concerto."

" So I hear. . . . Well, I am going home. It is too damned hot, and I've drunk too much sherry. Mind you don't sell that sherry. You just give it to me before the bailiffs arrive. I'll take care of it. You have probably killed your youngest son, but that is a better fate than would otherwise overtake him at the hands of American parents! Much better off dead. Good night," cheerfully. And he went home.

By now Arthur was seated at the piano, and Thibaud was tuning his violin. No lights turned on over the music-stands this time. The room had never been so quiet.

And then it began. Arthur became an orchestra, building with the sound of singing strings, resonant billowing brass, soft clear-blown wood and accurately thudding drums, a structure of needed volume for the single melodic unity of Thibaud's violin. In the unlighted corner of the studio, they played the work through, without slip or unwritten pause. Needless to say, they had never played it together before. Arthur had never played it at all. And yet no phrase of that immeasurably full work was scanted. Together they had given us the Brahms violin concerto from memory!

So Thibaud did play that night, after all. The performance stimulated a desire for more music. Casals suggested a Brahms sextet, the earlier one in B flat major. Thibaud was too exhausted from his inspired labours to play the first violin, so Paul Kochanski assumed the responsibility. Casals, his usually imperturbable serenity shaken in strange places by the concerto and the elusive unrest that pervaded Edith Grove that night, insisted upon taking Thibaud's violin, holding it low between his knees in place of his cherished cello (a position in which it could not remain for long at a time), and playing the second violin. It was an erratic performance. Tertis and Monteux played viola, Rubio and Felix Salmond the cellos. Even Rubio was affected, reaching over to poke Casals in the ribs with his bow when it was not in use, tears of laughter in his eyes at the sight of his " Pablissimo " turned violinist. Salmond could not have played badly, though he made a pretence of it, with occasional elaborate bowings which failed to mar the lovely flowing of his sure phrases. In spite of these unaccustomed indignities, Brahms emerged whole, and the sextet was enjoyably completed. The faithful Watson having manœuvred his double-bass into the house that afternoon and Eugene Goossens' two brothers both present, the Beethoven septet came next. At its close, Monteux was tempted out of his smiling taciturnity into witty and subtle imitation of Sir Thomas Beecham rehearsing the orchestra at Drury Lane. He repeated the only *mot* I ever heard of Nijinsky's, which was occasioned by his watching Sir Thomas from the wings one night, and exclaiming, " *Comme l'or-*

205

chestre dirige bien Monsieur Beecham *çe soir."* Without the generosity of this *Monsieur* Beecham, the orchestra might not have played *çe soir,* or any other evening — a fact of which dear Monteux was in no wise insensible.

Paul sang Schumann's *Dichter Liebe* cycle entire, and never sang more beautifully. His face and hands became as poignantly interpretive as his voice in order to give us that moving history of love.

Morning light came down into the studio. It was time for breakfast. We went up to the dining-room and began anew the ritual of breaking eggs and lighting coffe per-colators. The smell of fresh raspberries and pungent waking stocks mingled pleasurably.

Arbos, who has since become the distinguished con-ductor of the Madrid Symphony Orchestra, diverted us vastly by a very funny story of an unfortunate cornetist, who was forcibly prevented from coming in on the proper beat in a performance of Beethoven's *Leonora Over-ture* by the misinformed diligence of a new janitor, who, finding him in his right place outside the door lead-ing to the stage, instrument raised to his lips, thought he was practising his cornet by himself and made every at-tempt to check the disturbance. Arbos' enactment of the scene, with the violent gestures which such a situation would bring about, the frantic silence of the musician and the well-articulated fulminations of the over-zealous jani-tor, the puzzled rage of the conductor, was inimitable. He is a really witty person, and that rare thing, a born *raconteur.* Coffee boiled over as we listened and laughed: only Chester dabbled with the raspberries.

Sylvia Sparrow, a fair young English girl who danced about Edith Grove with wisplike vigor and played the violin exceedingly well, discussed a problem of phrasing of the Brahms violin concerto with Paul Kochanski. She had worked with Albert Sammons and Kochanski and was progressing eagerly toward fine accomplishments. They began to " sing " the phrase in question, and as violinists' voices belong in the category of pianists' and composers', I urged them out of our hearing and down into the studio, there to settle it or not, as best they could.

A few of us breakfasted in desultory fashion. Paul found it was time to change his clothes and pack his bags, or miss the train on which his voyaging to Germany would start, so he began his farewells. The party broke up.

Paul and I stood in the morning sunlight that spread itself over the threshold of No. 19. Chester puffed by us, patting his white gloves and saying, from a face wreathed in smiles, " You're crazy, you two: that's the only trouble with you — you're crazy! " When he reached the sidewalk, he looked up at the window of Paul Jr.'s bedroom to wave a white-gloved " Good Morning " to the burnished gold head that appeared in it, and padded heavily down the street, sending back a faint echo of " Tum, *ta*-ta-tumm, — ta, TUMM " through the early air.

Thibaud rushed down the steps, his chopped black locks falling over his face, waving his violin case in frightening carelessness, and calling out, " *Où est mon orchestre? Où est mon orchestre? Il me faut mon orchestre. Je ne peux pas partir sans mon orchestre: C'est une habitude.*"

207

His *orcheſtre* was closing the door of a taxi (taxis bloomed suddenly in the ſtreet where no taxis grew before, when Arthur wanted one), but upon hearing this flattering appeal, opened it and allowed Thibaud and his wildly waving violin to enter. They drove off together.

The two conduѐtors, Monteux and Arbos, went off arm in arm, an almoſt painful howl of laughter from the former a signal that the latter had not relinquished his rôle. Rubio blew us a kiss and took his adored Pablissimo to his lodgings around the corner, there to reveal to him the miraculous values of some newly acquired maſter-piece. Sozia and Paul Kochanski, lovely hard-working slim Sylvia between them, made off across the ſtreet to the little house in Edith Grove they had taken for the sea-son. Paul and I were left alone. He picked up the morn-ing papers from the ſteps and we went into the house. More bags were ſtill to be packed, the train yet to be caught, and German audiences in Germany to be convinced.

With the help of the miracle maids and the Irish angel, the moment of departure finally arrived. Paul telephoned Mühlen for a laſt word of encouragement and advice, said good-bye to Paul Jr., and the quite successfully weaned Smudge, kissed me rather crossly (he was begin-ning to want *not* to go) . . . and left for Germany.

At that moment, it would have been difficult to per-suade us that blood let flow from the veins of a murdered Archduke in Auſtria would flood the world between us before we met again.

* * * * * * * *

I undressed and went to bed, and made an attempt to go to sleep which was unsuccessful; so I rang the bell and ordered a regular morning breakfaſt, thinking it would give me the delusion of having slept, and began to read the papers. The situation in Ireland was becoming ſteadily worse. How much longer would conversations, conventions, and commissions avail againſt a country that was ſtanding to arms? England would solve the problem in time, with all the accuſtomed skill she could bring to bear on like entanglements, but at present it looked uncommonly like a crisis that was beyond the aid of diplomacy. However, the Auſtrian Archduke would be buried in a few days; the court mourning would be over; this troubled time would pass, and all would be serene once more . . . I needed my breakfaſt, which had been brought to my bedside.

A minute later, I was surprised to hear Douglas' voice shouting subversive admonitions to my sons from the ſtaircase. Presently he ſtood in the doorway of my bedroom. He inquired the lateſt news of the Brahms violin concerto: was it over? — because if not, he would leave the house until it was. I reassured him, and asked what the devil brought him to Edith Grove at that time in the morning.

" Well, there's that sherry, you know. The bailiffs are early risers," he answered. " Did Paul really leave for Germany? What did he go for? Very foolish of you to let him go."

" Why, Doug! what's the matter with you this morning? I know we were all a bit hyſterical laſt night, but

209

I don't expect you to be affected by such things. Why shouldn't Paul go to Germany? Mühlen wanted him to go. He is singing better than he ever sang in his life, and will probably make some money."

"Well, it's none of my business. Let's have some sherry. . . Is he going to Austria? "

"He doesn't expect to, thought he might possibly go to Vienna. He would like to make an arrangement to sing next season with the orchestra there, but I doubt if that can come about yet. However, he may try."

"Don't let him get killed in the rioting that's going on there. They are a little annoyed, you know. The man who shot their tiresome Archduke the other day has not been caught and punished yet. Not that they give a damn, but now that there has been a murder they want a good hanging to add to the sport. Paul looks rather like a murderer, don't you think? Where's the sherry? "

"I don't drink sherry at this time in the morning, and if you are trying to wish Paul into a murderer so he will be mobbed and killed in Vienna, in order to drink his sherry here in London, I will have it boiled and dropped slowly onto your — "

"Still in a bad temper, aren't you, Mew? " he interrupted. "Drink your nasty coffee then, and give me the papers." I handed them to him, and he retired to a corner of the room to read them. As I drank my coffee in sulky silence, he said from behind the papers, " You can always count on the stupidity of human beings."

This was a statement I did not feel prepared to argue. The irritating crackling of paper as he turned the leaves was the only sound in the room, until one of the miracle maids appeared with a note. I took it, opened it, and read the following:

> 5, Netherton Grove
> Chelsea, S. W.
> July 3rd, 1914

DEAR MADAM:

I am writing in behalf of my neighbours, viz., Mr. and Mrs. St. John Hare, Miss Kennington, Mr. and Mrs. Muckle [1] and myself, all residing in Netherton Grove, at the back of Edith Grove, to ask you to refrain, in future, from playing the piano all night. On June 25th, you played from midnight to 4 o'clock in the morning. On the 28th, playing began after 10 & we still heard it at 6:30. Last night, July 2nd, playing went on till after 3 in the morning.

Now that all windows have to be open, I can assure you that you might be playing in the next room, and sleep becomes quite impossible. I would therefore ask you to have all playing in the evening stopped at a reasonable hour, as we are all of us early people and I am sure you will quite understand how very trying it is to be defrauded of our night's rest.

> Believe me,
> Yours truly,
> J. OSTREROG.

The threatening dilemma of J. Ostrerog and his neighbours presented itself as a welcome break in the nervous

[1] No relation to May!

monotony of the morning: it furnished a cause, however slight, for angry indulgence of my nerves and drove me to action. I showed it to Douglas and announced my intention of taking it to a lawyer at once. The anonymous disapproval previously voiced by policemen's whistles, torpedoes, and rattles was all very well, but a written, signed document asking us to "refrain" was more serious, and I determined to discover whether music could be stopped by law. Douglas was supremely disinterested: he gathered up his papers and left the room, agreeing to wait somewhere about in the house until my return to hear the verdict, provided he could sip a glass of sherry.

I dressed and hurried to my benevolent and all-wise solicitors, Messrs. Hunt and Money (such inspired names!), who decided, in the engaging terminology of Anglo-Saxon law, that it was a "frivolous objection" which could not be maintained and that we had only to take ourselves and all our guests to court and repeat any one of the accused performances to prove our innocence in the eyes of the judge. The thought of Casals, Rubinstein, Thibaud, and Tertis playing a Brahms quartet, followed by Draper singing the *Winterreise* before an English judge in an English court-room, as evidence that it did not constitute a public nuisance, so tempted me that I longed to bring it about. In any case it put me in a good humour, and I returned to Edith Grove ready to discuss the stupidity of human beings, or prove with fervour the intelligence of American parents.

I found Douglas still immersed in the morning papers,

and in no vein for anything but lunch, which we ate
peacefully enough, with no further reference to murderers
or sherry. Never before or since, however, have I known
Norman Douglas in just that mood. He left soon after
lunch, and I went up to my room, and sleep, at last.

. . . .

For a short, strange while Time held its breath. Nights
flowed quietly into days at Edith Grove. Chester brought
a book to my eldest son. Von zur Mühlen came laden
with the flowers of his garden. Arthur Rubinstein shaped
life in the sound of music. Rubio paused in his pursuit of
masterpieces: the Kochanskis crossed the street daily in
ever-welcome neighbourliness. Casals was gone in search
of his romance. Thibaud was in France. Karol Sczymanowski wanted to go home to Poland. Baroness von Hutten and I ate plovers' eggs and discussed our children,
and mine were happy. Whithorne was ill and confused
by the conflicting attentions of enamoured ladies who
hovered about his bedside: the situation was simplified by
his moving into Edith Grove, where he recuperated in
peace. The bailiffs were patient, and I still went to the
Russian ballet in my own motor.

The last performance of the season was announced
for Saturday, July twenty-fifth. Sozia, Paul Kochanski,
Arthur, Karol, and I dined together at home, and went
on to it in excited sadness. Never again could there be
such a season, and this was the last night of it. The
audience at Drury Lane was spread out in a brilliant
peacock's-tail gesture of farewell, courting a return of the
romantically deluded delights that danced into reality

before it. On this last night, the colour structure of splendid red-violet gold and white, bright steady blue and silver, hot yellow-orange and scarlet against cool green, that had been flung up on the remote stage, fell across the black and white and metal restraint of the orchestra, and out into our lives through our eyes. Sound that had vibrated into shapes of differing intensity and rhythm broke from the moulds that had formed it and invaded the air we breathed. Moving bodies came to rest in us as the heavy curtain closed. Some sat receiving these gifts, some stood to balance them. The noise of hands struck against each other and throats shutting and opening on shouts grew into clapping and calling.

" Bravo! Nijinsky! — Diaghilev! Bravo! "

" Monteux — Nijinsky — Chaliapin! Bravo!! "

" Karsavina — brava brava! "

" Diaghilev — Nijinsky — Chaliapin — Brav-O-O! Brav-O-O-O!! "

" Bra — Nijinsk — O!   *Bra* — hilev — sky — O! Diagh — jinsk — brrraaa — o-o-o-o-o-o. . . ."

Lights went dark and bright again . . . and a dim pink voice behind me said, putting each tired word neatly into my ear, " Here you all are, like birds of paradise — none of you realizing the thing that is hanging over your heads."

I turned and saw Sir Claude Phillips, his face like a dusty, unsmiling cherub, his demeanour very grave. I had never seen him so.

" Why, Sir Claude! angel. What is wrong? Why shouldn't we look like birds of paradise? Don't you

like it? What is hanging over our heads? You mean this
Auftrian business — this note to Serbia? "

(" Bravo! Brav-O! BRAvo!!! Diagh — jinsk —
Diagh — ")

" You'll know when it falls, my dear, and soon
enough. It's no longer juft ' this Auftrian business.' . . .
Are you going to M. Cambon's? " And he smiled a small
smile under his little finger, crooked to scratch the tip
of his nose. Reassured by the familiar gefture, I answered:

" Yes — that is, if this ominous thing that is hanging
over our heads doesn't fall before I get there. You coming
too? "

" Yes — I'll see you there." He turned and walked
loosely away, his rare waves of hair looking limp and
long on the back of his head.

Sir Claude's few sentences had made me gather up
the magic of the night in some confusion, and hold it
close as the Kochanskis, Arthur and I moved out of the
box. Drury Lane became a big, half-empty theatre as we
walked through it. The lights did not come bright again.

.   .   .   .

We went on to the house of the Ambassador from
France, M. Paul Cambon, who was giving a party. He
received us with his peculiarly alert grace. Did I imagine
it to be caught under a barely perceptible network of fine
anxiety? After greeting him I watched him. His closely
woven, fturdily small body looked nervous, and his
white-fringed, quickly moving head paused a second or
two longer than usual at a name here and there.

Amongft the hundreds that were crowding the rooms,

I wanted to find Sir Claude. I was told he was in one of the big salons upstairs, where *The Blessed Damozel* was being performed or recited or enacted or whatever happens about such things. It was to be — indeed, was being, according to report — an extraordinary happening. I did not want to see it, but I did want to see Sir Claude. I went upstairs. At the top of the staircase stood a laughing woman who said to a man, " Yes, in a black dress. *Really*. All the rest are in white."

She was laughing as I passed her and started across a large drawing-room in the direction of closed doors at the opposite end. The furniture in this room became smaller and smaller as I passed it on a longer and longer journey. Would the room never end? The far away closed doors moved slightly and toward me, without noise, and the busy little figure of Paul Reimers squeezed through them in polite quiet, a chord of music slipping in with him before the doors closed again silently. He began a journey too. We travelled toward each other through Time. When there was only a century or two of tiny chairs and tables between us, he put a short finger up beside his gay red and gold face and whispered across to me, " It's such a *jolly* little party, isn't it? " and trotted busily on into space behind me. I called after him not to leave me, but as in all nightmares, he did not heed me. I was alone in that room once more. And I decided that, — be damozels blessed or cursed, be Sir Claude possessed of all the information of the world (not just of " this Austrian business "), — I would go home. I made the return journey of the room, the staircase (the

lady still laughing), the doorway, the air, in as miraculously short a time as the advance had been long. No
good nights. I was in the motor. I was in Edith Grove.
I was in bed. My head was free of the turbans and feathers
and earrings, but heavy under the overhanging thing.
I held the magic of the night close, safe from its threat.

.   .   .   .

Monday, the twenty-seventh of July. The London
season of 1914 was over.

I had taken a small house by the sea, and had planned
to spend the months of August and September there with
the two sons and the Irish angel, leaving the miracle
maids in charge of Edith Grove until its fate and mine
should be decided. The motor was to carry us there on its
last trip at the end of the week. For the first time since
the shooting at Sarajevo, the European situation was
occupying the leading position in the London papers.
Serbia had replied to the Austria-Hungarian note. Douglas was right about the stupidity of human beings. Why
make all this fuss about a murder? Surely Sir Claude
was wrong: England could not be mixed up in it.

The week passed quickly. Friends sat about while
packing went on. The possibilities of war between Austria
and Serbia were discussed casually. And then suddenly
it was no longer a possibility. It was a fact. A declaration
of war was issued at Vienna against Serbia. (How could
I get that enormous perambulator to the seaside? Couldn't
take it in the motor. Perhaps it could be left behind.)
There had been some shooting in Dublin. How nervous
people were! (Yes, tell him to cut off the water, unless

you need it. Why, of course you'll need it. Mr. Draper?
No. Yes. I don't know. All right.) Suggestions took the
place of conversations. Sir Edward Grey was being very
polite. The chauffeur was being very polite too. Friday
morning at ten? No, better make it Friday afternoon at
three.

So, Friday afternoon at three we started off, leaving
the perambulator behind. Douglas stood on the steps of
19 Edith Grove to say good-bye, informing me that I
would get no further than the corner before he would be
at the sherry. The miracle maids stood behind him,
listening in unsmiling delight. We left for the seaside.
. . . We arrived. I have no picture in my mind of that
little house. I know the ocean was just beyond it. I see
vaguely the figure of a kind, worried little woman who
welcomed us, and spoke of tea. The Irish angel took
charge. The children were tired and cross. Someone
brought the papers. The evening news was alarming. It
looked at last as if the inconceivable thing might happen.
Where was Paul? I told the chauffeur not to go back to
London yet — to wait somewhere — to wait. . . .

Saturday. Russia mobilized. Germany under martial
law. The kind little woman made very bad coffee. Nothing would come out of my trunk. Paul Jr. had left his
Golliwog at Edith Grove. . . . How could I get it? The
water was shut off? The sea was nearer than the night before. Perhaps I could reach Paul by cable. Sir Edward
Grey, speaking for England, was still desperately polite.
Sunday would be calmer, somehow.

No. It was less calm. German troops were actually

in France. That violated some treaty or other. Britain was finally involved. Yes, it was Sunday and Britain was involved. Sir Claude was right after all. It was not only hanging over our heads, it was at our throats — a very different feeling. It was a bad dream. Monday was the beginning of a new week. I would wake up and find everything right again. If only these ambassadors would stop going home!

And the new week began, with five nations of the world unaccountably at war. The papers reported that in London the Cabinet had been in practically continuous session over Sunday. No decision yet. Merely involved.

The chauffeur appeared in the dining-room of the little cottage while I was at breakfast, and asked if he should wait any longer. The car was outside. I said, " No. I am going up myself. We will leave at once," and I got up from the breakfast table, stepped into the car, and we left, the Irish angel calling out after me, " Ma*dame,* you've no hat . . . " I had no hat.

. . . .

In every town I passed through on the way up to London, the flaring little placards posted up outside the newstands flashed grim information in great black letters. "BRITISH NAVAL RESERVES MOBILIZED." . . . "ITALY REMAINS NEUTRAL." (It was her own business, of course, but . . .) " At meeting of French Chamber, the Government will be asked to state attitude of Great Britain." (What *was* the attitude of Great Britain?) " German Ambassador reported to be leaving Paris to-night." Everybody was going home. Where was Paul?

Edith Grove at laſt. The ſtocks were ſtill blooming in the window boxes, which seemed very ſtrange. Everywhere blinds were drawn down, save in the two kitchen windows. I walked up the ſteps and rang the bell, and marvelled when the door was opened. The two dear, faithful women I had left there so long ago showed no surprise at my return. No, there was no news of Mr. Draper. Yes, the water and eleƈtricity could be turned on at once. Maſter Paul's Golliwog? Oh, yes! Madam. Put away in camphor in the nursery closet. Lunch? Yes, Madam . . . if Madam would like a kippered herring? I liked it. And then I began to telephone. Nothing really definite yet. Not even at the American Embassy. People arrived, newspapers under their arms. The house became unbearable. We went out into the ſtreets. Many other people were in the ſtreets, which nevertheless appeared indescribably empty. We trailed along the King's Road. . . . We were in front of Buckingham Palace. I turned down the Mall toward the Houses of Parliament, saying I would meet the others for dinner in the grill of the Hyde Park Hotel. I telegraphed Paul. I bought more papers. France ſtill wanted to know. I sent telegrams to the children. I went to see von zur Mühlen, though I knew he was in Steyning. So the afternoon passed, and I made my way to the Hyde Park Hotel. In the grill were more friends. (" Well, my dear, I can only tell you that his orders are to cross water. Yes, to cross water." . . .) We dined. There was some difficulty about a five-pound note in payment of dinner. Difficulty about a five-pound note in England! . . . We went back to Edith Grove.

Douglas came in during the evening. " What are you all so glum about? A little war won't do anyone any harm. Far too many people in the world as it is, most of them stupid."

Arthur Rubinstein came in and proceeded to play with one finger the shepherd's motif from *Tristan and Isolde* until I begged him to stop. A German gentleman and his lovely English wife, who were dearly loved friends of ours, appeared. We were all excessively cordial to them — to him in particular.

I do not remember sleeping that night, but waking on Tuesday morning is clear. The house seemed full of people. They just had not gone home. Only ambassadors went home. No, some Americans were going home too. They could not get into hotels, so crowded had London suddenly become, and for some reason they slept at Edith Grove. I cannot remember their names. . . . More Americans were going home — rushing home, in fact. Where was Paul? I telephoned the American Embassy again. They would try to reach him.

Out into the streets again. They were less empty to-day. It was Tuesday, the fourth of August, 1914. The German Ambassador had left Paris the night before, as reported. The French Ambassador, M. Jules Cambon, was to leave Berlin at once. He was the brother of M. Paul Cambon, who had given " such a *jolly* little party " for birds of paradise on an enchanted night a thousand years ago. The vacillating suspense felt the day before was changing hourly into resolute tumult. The cries of newsboys were raucous with excitement. France was not asking any more. She must have been answered. Another telephone to the American Embassy vouchsafed no further news of Paul, but a suggestion that it would be wise to take the children away from the sea, and bring them back to London. I wired the Irish angel at once, and she brought them safely home under her wing. Paul Jr. was too blissfully happy in the recovery of his Golliwog to question this change of plan. Smudge was too young.

I sat with them through supper, and saw them to bed. They soon slept, and I began to telephone again. I could talk to people at that distance, but I did not want to see anyone. I went out into the streets again.

The eyes of men and women looked anxiously dazzled. I wondered if a 'bus conductor would change a shilling. The head waiter had been very odd about five-pound notes. Money had become so trivial, and yet one had to get somewhere. I would walk. . . .

Again I was in front of the Houses of Parliament. To-night it was different. There were more people, less noise; yet there was no stillness, only a concrete waiting. Then, in a bad new moment, a moment that had not been in the world before, the waiting broke into knowing. It was known that England was at war. I knew England was at war. It happened like that: England was at war.

· · · · · · · ·

The crowd became more people than there were in the world. They made much noise; a low, pleased, loose, rumbling noise and a mockingly high, tight, wrangling noise. Some of it became singing. They sang the *Marseillaise*. Each person was moved by those next him: we all moved together and toward Buckingham Palace. A distorted face tore through the compactness, shouting, " Buy a flag! Buy a flag! *Buy a flag,* won'tcher? " It frightened me. I gave the man the shilling. I did not take his flag. I like them moving in the air, not held in the hand. It was all the same to him. He spread more people apart, repeating his angry command. We closed in after him and got nearer to Buckingham Palace. We came to some red geraniums and stopped. They looked no more red than green under the light. I shouldered past them and got still nearer to Buckingham Palace. The noise became a proud, unified roar. The waiting began again, but it was eager: it was purposeful. I was pressed against closed iron gates. Through them, across the vast dim, empty forecourt of the Palace, I saw the remote shape of a man move separately from other shapes on a balcony. Now there was stillness, and the people of England had been told by their King that they were at war. I heard not a sound until the air burst with cheers that drained off into sobs underneath. The crowd broke into pieces which started slowly away. Men and women walked out of these pieces alone in different directions. One of them, a tiny bent woman who looked very old, darted crazily over to one of the high closed iron gates. She sprang at it, clutching the iron bars and climbing up them until she reached the top. There she clung, tremblingly, her little dark garments flapping around her. Watching her, people became a crowd again. Finally steadying herself, she stretched her small, black-hatted old head over the top of the gate, and in an insecure and terribly shrill voice began to sing *God Save the King*, sending the cracked notes out across the echoing forecourt in anguished determination. No one sang with her. Had they done so she would not have heard them. She was clinging alone to the gates of a palace and singing.

I went home.

. . . .

My sons were sleeping. Their guardian angel was praying. Nectarines were in a silver bowl by my bedside. If it had not been for the irreproachable character of those two maids, I should have been sure it was stolen fruit. Whithorne was wandering about. John McMullin was eating a horrible compilation of food he had extracted from the ice chest, and trying to scold me for having been in the streets alone. Douglas was asleep in a big armchair in the studio, and made no attempt at gaiety when he woke. Mrs. Napier telephoned. Arthur Rubinstein came in with more newspapers. I could not look at them. The American Embassy telephoned: they had not been able to reach Paul. For the moment, he was nowhere in the world. England was at war.

. . . .

The months passed. Men went away and women missed them. When they did not come back, women were brave. When they did, people were glad.

Everyone was very busy. Even I cut out clumsy pyjamas in a strange place. The aspect of the streets changed.

Men walked in uniforms of varying splendour. Olive-green-grey-covered trucks, with solid red crosses evenly painted on their sides, delivered broken human bodies at doors of big houses. One stepped carefully in the aisles of theatres to avoid stumbling over crutches. Food was different. There was often a little laughter. No one complained. They worked and read the papers, worked and waited for the next edition — and then waited for the next day. The war would be over by Christmas: the war would last twelve years. . . . This is not a history of the war.

Paul Draper made his hazardous way out of Germany and appeared in the entrance of the studio at Edith Grove one September day, while the American Embassy was still trying to reach him. He was dazed by unhappy surprise, and worn from the effort of realizing what was taking place amongst people who had written the most beautiful songs in the world. His mother had died since his departure, and he left almost immediately for America.

I stayed in England. The words of the great French poet no longer availed, and I had to do something. I mortgaged the furniture: no one was buying any. An odd dark man in a warehouse filled with empty coaches and carriages gave me what seemed a huge sum of money for it: at swiftly recurring intervals I gave much of it back to him — interest, it was called. (Interest. How did that word ever come to mean that?) No one ate much, but children must not eat less. Pawnshops were convenient banks. Feathers and turbans did not bring much, but

pearl bridles and earrings brought more. Frocks were
no good at all — who would wear them where? But
on very dreary days they were pleasant to put on.
Friends lunched and dined together, and when men
came back, danced together; but there were no " parties," exactly.

.   .   .   .

Christmas came and went. It was 1915. It was truly
a new year that had never been used before. Perhaps the
bad new moment that had come into the world at eleven
o'clock on the night of August 4, 1914, had been bor-
rowed from this year.

There were concerts. The London public did not
deafen its ears with accidents of climate and biology.
For one week there was a festival of the music of Bach,
Brahms and Beethoven in Queen's Hall, conducted by a
German. Some people stoutly and smilingly averred that
he was Dutch, but they listened and enjoyed. There was
enough fighting to do in the war: they did not need
to bring it into other places. The necessarily diligent
tracking down of spies had produced, to be sure, an
overflow of hysterical accusations and precautions. The
mistakes that ensued were as often comic as tragic. Hordes
of Russian soldiers, armed to the teeth, were " seen "
behind blinds in innocent country trains, riding north,
east, south and west at the same time. Tales of the mon-
strousness of the enemy that rose out of waves of horror
during the more prolonged absences of the men who were
fighting it, fell to calmer levels upon their return. Flee-
ing, boring Belgians were settling down for life in Eng-

land with a complacence that was as humorous as it was surprising.

We made music in Edith Grove. Thibaud brought Ysaye one night. I heard him come grumbling down the staircase into 19A before I saw him, Thibaud keeping up a conciliatory chatter behind. When he stepped into the room, he stood blinking his slow eyes and wavering like a distinguished bear on its hind legs. Then he crossed the room to where I waited to greet him, and smiling beautifully, flung out his arms and said,

" *Mais, c'est géniale, votre cave, madame.* "

I did not dare suggest his playing that night, knowing he had crossed the Channel that very day, and being a little warily conscious of his wife's watchful eye. You have to be careful of musicians' wives. The only one I did not have to be beware of was myself.

Thibaud played a Mozart sonata with Arthur, and when Warwick Evans, Albert Sammons, Waldo Warner, and Lionel Tertis arrived an hour later, they played the Brahms piano and string quartet in C Minor. Ysaye wept with pleasure at this performance. It is a perfect work. His wife eyed him out of the house after his first glass of champagne (the cellar was not yet empty), fairly early in the evening. He blinked wisely at me, and with a gallant salutation, said,

" *Je reviendrai, madame. Je vous adore, et c'est vraiment géniale, votre cave. La prochaine fois j'y apporterai mon violon!* "

He kept his word.

. . . .

227

At times one lived through days and nights in a dead, weary excitement of nothing beyond waiting for news, and reading it when it came. We sat about in chairs, turning the pages of White Papers, Blue Papers, and newspapers. One could hold each ſtep of the terrible progression ſteadily separate for days at a time, and then suddenly all in a minute they would fall heedlessly together in a shuffled meaninglessness. A thing in this heap grew conſtantly greater: it was a thing of men insanely killing each other. The next minute would bring a new set of events so brave as to cheat your eyes and mind away from the sight of this thing, and the whole miserable thing would begin over again.

Families and friends begged and commanded me to return to America. It was as impossible to do as it was difficult to explain: I would not leave England. A siſter of mine who lived there with her husband, watched me quietly — obviously not daring to say how much she wanted me to ſtay — and loyally tried to persuade me to go home.

There was in London at this time an important old American woman who had known me since the earlier days in Florence. There, she had brought jars of meat-broth to my bedside a day or two after the birth of my eldeſt son and finding Lily Braggiotti there, had fought bravely with her as to whether a young nursing mother should or should not imbibe such poison — had fought and won, turning to Lily with a " I don't care whether you've nursed a whole orphan asylum on a diet of onions, Muriel Draper is going to have this broth! " Troubled and well-meaning friends in America had sent her as an ambassador of sorts on a visit to Edith Grove. She sat with me before lunch in a little drawing-room that opened into the dining-room. She found me obstinately impervious to any cajolery or advice she had to offer. Her observant old eyes took in every detail of the house, the movements of people in and out of it, the room, my clothes and myself, though the essence of the situation escaped her. She went away defeated. Meat-broth for a nursing mother was all very well, but America for the human being I was in that certain time was not. . . . I month after her visit, I received an indignant letter from America, saying, " Mrs. X—— writes us that she made a visit to Edith Grove and found the goose hanging high. The awnings were up, the flowers blooming in the window boxes; your baby slept in his carriage in the garden. A maid opened the door. You were on a sofa in a lace tea-gown, and, by the looks of the dining-table, it was obvious that people were expected for lunch! How *can* this be if you are without funds in a country that is at war ? "

How could it, indeed? I should have burned the awnings, I suppose, torn up the flowers by the roots, kept my baby awake in the cellar with toy guns and drums, banished the servants into the streets where they would be without food as well as wages, sent my lace tea-gown to the Red Cross for bandages, and locked my door in the face of those who brought food and friendship to my table. Yes — and my father should not have turned Boston into an enchanted city for me with ten ones.

229

So I stayed in Edith Grove. Douglas came almost daily, sometimes bringing chops and cheese, and never mentioning sherry. Whithorne, morose and devoted, would walk with me through Richmond Park, or together we would shake about on the top of a 'bus bound for Crouch End or Stroud Green, the very depression of such names affording some relief to our strained nerves. Mrs. Napier and I drank many a cup of tea together in Edith Grove, her undimmed blue eyes watching me with penetrating kindness, her tactful lips never framing the anxiety she felt for my welfare, sifting her wit unfailingly through her heart, before allowing it to be used by her quick mind. Her brother, General Munro, was at the front, so she brought fresh news. Chester puffed and hummed, and was content in the society of my two sons, who were naturally enough less affected than the rest of us by the disasters that befell the world in which we lived. In a moment of inspired wisdom, John McMullin brought a young man who made hats out of feather dusters and faded window curtains. For a day, he sat cross-legged on the Chinese daybed in a corner of the studio, and unperturbed by wars and rumours of wars, fashioned lovely nonsense to put on my head. Nobody but John could have thought of just that distraction. It infuriated Rubinstein so that he left for Russia, preferring death to such indignity. Unfortunately, he could not get across the Russian frontier, and might better have borne with millinery for a day, for he had only to come back again.

E. Grant Watson, who had been part of the conspiracy to prevent Gertrude Stein's too personal use of the word

" chair," looked very stern and splendid when he first appeared in uniform. The lonely German friend who had married a lovely English wife happened to be there on that day, and, alas! in a nervous attempt to prove how little susceptible he was to the outward and visible sign of an enmity he did not feel, did a supremely insensitive thing. He put E. Grant Watson's cap on his own head, saying, " How do I look in it? "

Watson leaped at him in a quick, impersonal rage, shouting,

" TAKE THAT HAT OFF! "

The German took it off. Two of the mildest men I have ever seen, they faced each other in utter astonishment — on the one hand, that such a gesture should have been made, and on the other, that it should have been so received. If men became deaf, dumb, and blind for the instant they met in battle, could they kill? . . .

One fair day in May, I made a last visit to the odd dark gentleman who sat over the carriage warehouse. He whistled a little tune while I made cabalistic signs on a slip of pink paper and handed it to him. Interest again. He thanked me and I thanked him. I walked by the empty coaches and out in the lovely May day again. On the way home, I realized that the slip of pink paper was the last exchangeable value I had in the world. It had been made clear to me that from America would come the wherewithal to return there, but nothing else. There was no work I could do in London that would support me and my two sons. I had to make a decision.

Arrived at Edith Grove, I found Douglas waiting there.

He saw that I was in desperate perplexity, and suggested our walking over Battersea Bridge to his flat, where he would show me some correspondence that would amuse and surprise me, after which he would cook me a meal. " Put on one of those terrible hats that little —— made for you and come along." What a civilized man! His instincts are rooted deep in sanity: his intellectual curiosity brings him fearless use of them. If his despair of " the stupidity of human beings " makes him flagrantly indifferent to their judgments, his knowledge of their lost possibilities for wisdom makes him respect his own. Life has left him lazily contemptuous, not working him enough, but can never take from him the isolated integrity of againstment he so cheerily maintains. So I put on one of those terrible hats and started away with him, across Battersea Bridge.

On the way, he ducked into a greengrocer's shop for a minute, to buy the most lively cheese he could find: he declared this taste of mine for corrupt cheese to be my only hope against the ænemic passion I displayed for vegetables. I waited for him outside and noticed a pale pink poster on a near-by news stand. On it I saw in black letters: " L, U, S, I, T, A, N, I, A, S, U, N, K." For the thousandth of a second after it meant nothing more to me than that: the letters, L, U, S, I, T, A, N, I, A, S, U, N, K, in black on faded pink. Had this to do with those other letters on pink earlier in the day? Confused thoughts of the *Titanic:* a mistake in name — a crazy newsdealer — a crazy me — ran up and down each other and then, as Norman came out of the shop and toward me, I said,

" Look, Doug," and pointed to the placard. When I heard my words, " Look, Doug," I knew that a ship called the *Lusitania* had been sunk. A second after, he knew it, though he, too, experienced that infinitesimal pause of unresponse. Then we continued our way across Battersea Bridge to his flat, where he showed me the surprising correspondence, and cooked me an excellent meal. . . . And I decided to go back to America. After which he took me home.

.   .   .   .

It was all so dizzily sad and easy, once I had made my decision and communicated it. I went through the business of passports and tickets and cables and payments quite mechanically, and there was nothing further to do but wait to go. I waited to go. The pull of my resisting body was not enough to keep the days and nights from flying through time with lunatic speed, until one of the days stopped long enough for me to know it was the last one. I was leaving England the next day. Clothes and golliwogs were packed. I gave Douglas the sherry at last. Everything else was just as it always beautifully had been. We were to have one last party in Edith Grove that night.

The children were asleep. Douglas was with me. People arrived. Arthur, back from Russia, had come for dinner, which the miracle maids had created out of nothing. Ysaye, who had returned often to my *cave,* bringing his violin and, playing it with indestructible virtuousity, soon followed. The London String Quartet arrived. Barrere, in London by happy chance, hurried in with his flute. The rooms were filled with flowers from Mühlen's garden. I had said good-bye to him that morning. We went down to the studio. The electricity had been turned off weeks before, but the last of the huge church candles furnished us with light enough. The Goddess of Charity gleamed whitely under her golden canopy, and the little figures on the Kien Lung screen blazed. The cushions were piled high either side of the fireplace in which three carefully saved logs of wood burned. May nights are cool.

They began with the Mozart G Minor quartet, Sammons, Petrie, Warwick Evans and Waldo Warner playing it as even they had never played it before. Ysaye played the first movement of the Mozart E Minor sonata with Arthur. In these two works Mozart touched great tragedy in music. Sammons and Arthur followed with my favourite A Major violin sonata of Brahms, and then Arthur played Bach. . . . It was time for supper. We went up the staircase, bringing the lighted candles with us. The fact that I was leaving this in a few hours conveyed nothing to me, though I knew it well enough. The room smelled of stocks. We drank much coffee and ate strange little biscuits. Rows of small glasses filled with Rhubarb Fool stood on the sideboard. Doug had brought a stupendous cheese. We were very gay. The beloved Rubio had joined us, which made it possible to play the Schubert quintet, and we went back into the studio to begin it. They were giving me imperishable music.

After the quintet, Barrere, Ysaye, and Arthur played the exquisite serenade for violin, piano, and flute that is one of Beethoven's earliest and loveliest accomplishments. When it was over, Arthur played the Chopin B flat Sonata. It was Warwick Evans himself who suggested playing the second of Beethoven's Rasoumowsky quartets. It was getting undeniably late.

Ysaye was beginning to be very unhappy over the prospective loss of his *cave,* and Sammons was discussing tentatively the idea of bringing his quartet to America. . . . And then it was morning of the day I was to leave England. You could see it through the window in the roof.

I went upstairs to change my clothes, and found the children dressing and being dressed, Paul Jr. in a frenzy of excitement over going to America.

" What is it like, Mum? " he asked. " Is it like the Park? "

" No. No, it is not like the Park. It's like — well, it's America. You'll see," I answered, and shut a trunk.

The two maids were moving freshly about, and the Irish angel was pale from praying and packing. Douglas came upstairs and cheered her with ribaldries. He sat down with her and the children in the day nursery for breakfast, and God knows what parting advice.

I walked down and called the others from the studio for breakfast. We lighted the faithful old percolator once again, and broke eggs for the last time in the dining-room of Edith Grove. Arthur and I made a search in the kitchen for some butter to scramble them in, and discovered two small bottles of champagne and a little yellow terrine of paté-de-fois-gras. We pounced upon them and carried them back to the dining-room. Our breakfast was of eggs,

235

Douglas' stupendous cheese, coffee, a stray Rhubarb Fool, a shadow of champagne in our glasses, and a smear of paté on our bread.

The children were bustling downstairs, and trunks were bumping down after them, mysteriously summoned men carrying them out and putting them in taxicabs.

I went down into the studio alone. The fire was burning. One candle was not yet out. The piano was open and the parts of the Beethoven quartet were on the music-stands. In the morning light the flowers were lifting their heads, and on the tables violins and a flute were carefully laid. Smoke was curling up into the roof and the room was filled with sound. I left it so, and so it is.

. . . .

It was time to go. The children were in one of the taxis with Douglas and their guardian angel. The miracle maids were sobbing discreetly on the stairs. I said good-bye to my friends. Tears began to spurt out from under Ysaye's blinking eyes. I gave him the key to the house, telling him to come and bring all who would come with him, there to make music until no note could find a place. He took it, looked at it, and rushed down into the studio, coming back with his violin in his hand. I waved to them all, and walked through the door, out of 19 Edith Grove. With the magic I had held close since the night it was threatened, I drew a circle around the life I left there: as it closed, I heard music.

I turned to look. And there in the door they stood, Ysaye, Barrere, Rubio, Sammons, Warner, Petrie, and Evans, their instruments miraculously at hand, playing

236

divinely. I do not know what they played, but as it carried me across the sidewalk and into the waiting cab, I heard from the open window in the roof of 19A the splendid chords of the Hammer Klavier Sonata.

．　．　．　．　．　．　．　．

The golden era was at an end.

NEW YORK
Publishers of BOOKS and of
HARPER'S MAGAZINE
Established 1817